Strategy
in practice

Strategy
in practice

CLIFF BOWMAN

PRENTICE HALL EUROPE
LONDON ♦ NEW YORK ♦ TORONTO ♦ SYDNEY ♦ TOKYO ♦
SINGAPORE ♦ MADRID ♦ MEXICO CITY ♦ MUNICH ♦ PARIS

First published 1998 by
Prentice Hall Europe
Campus 400, Maylands Avenue
Hemel Hempstead
Hertfordshire, HP2 7EZ
A division of
Simon & Schuster International Group

Typeset in 10.5/13.5 Meridien
by Photoprint, Torquay, S. Devon

Printed and bound in Great Britain by
Biddles Ltd, Guildford and King's Lynn

Library of Congress Cataloging-in-Publication Data

Bowman, Cliff.
    Strategy in practice / Cliff Bowman.
        p. cm.
    Includes bibliographical references and index.
    ISBN 0–13–356486/X (alk. paper)
    1. Strategic planning. I. Title.
HD30.28.B687   1998
    658.4'012—dc21   97–42856
                                                  CIP

British Library Cataloguing in Publication Data

A catalogue record for this book is available from
the British Library

ISBN 0–13–356486–X

---

1 2 3 4 5   02 01 00 99 98

Contents

Preface *ix*

Chapter 1 **A sense of strategy** *1*
Introduction *1*
Levels of strategy *3*
Strategy processes *6*
Confidence in setting strategy *12*
The plan of the book *16*
So what? *18*

Chapter 2 **The customer matrix** *20*
Introduction *20*
The customer matrix *20*
Segments of demand *22*
Representing products on the matrix *22*
Cutting price *23*
Adding perceived use value *28*
What happens next? *30*
Other moves in the customer matrix *34*
Constructing the customer matrix *36*
So what? *40*
Summary *41*

Chapter 3 **Sustaining advantage** *42*
Effecting movements in the customer matrix *42*
Competitive imitation *43*
Resources, systems and know-how *48*
Reducing costs *56*
Adding value at low cost *59*
Crude cost-cutting *61*
Competing across segments *64*

Competitor actions and reactions *66*
So what? *67*
Summary *69*

Chapter 4 **The competitive environment** *70*
Drivers of demand *71*
Drivers of imitability *72*
Structural analysis of industries *74*
Rivalry *74*
Barriers to entry *77*
Bargaining power of buyers *79*
Bargaining power of suppliers *79*
Threat of substitutes *80*
Advantages of the five-forces framework *84*
Industry life cycle *85*
Interrelationships between the five forces *88*
Competitor analysis *92*
So what? *95*
Summary *97*

Chapter 5 **Strategy, structure and processes** *98*
Introduction *98*
Organizational structure: some basic concepts *98*
The five parts of the organization *103*
Organizational processes *103*
Linking strategy, structure and process *104*
The functional structure *104*
A "contingency" approach to strategy and structure *106*
Changes in the contingent variables *107*
Structural responses to changes in strategy and
    environment *114*
Coping with diversity *118*
So what? *119*
Summary *120*

Chapter 6 **Strategy and culture** *122*
Introduction *122*
Culture and strategy *124*
Organizational processes *126*
Grouping *127*
Power *128*

Controls and rewards *129*
Management styles *130*
Routines *132*
Stories and symbols *133*
Cognitive processes *135*
Behaviour *138*
Realized strategy and performance *139*
So what? *140*
Summary *143*

Chapter 7 **Managing strategic change** *145*
Culture and strategic change *145*
Content quality versus process quality *147*
Triggering change *147*
The mission statement *149*
Using the status quo to change the status quo *156*
Change processes *156*
Identifying barriers to change *159*
Prioritizing and ownership *161*
Building experience and self-confidence *165*
So what? *168*
Summary *170*

Chapter 8 **Corporate strategy** *172*
Creating value from the centre *172*
Selecting: should we diversify? *173*
Resourcing *175*
Selecting and resourcing: mergers and acquisitions *180*
Controlling: achieving synergies *183*
Strategy problems in not-for-profit organizations *185*
So what? *187*
Concluding comments *188*

Case study **S. J. Matthews** *190*

Further reading *198*

Index *199*

Preface

This book has been written for managers who have responsibility for strategy. It has evolved from *The Essence of Strategic Management*, which set out to address a need for a practical, concise and readable text for managers. The *Essence* book has been a great success, and has also found a market amongst MBA students who are looking for a brief but reliable introduction to the field of strategic management. An indicator of the appeal of the first book is that it has been translated into several languages, including Chinese and Japanese.

When I was asked by Prentice Hall to prepare a new edition of the book, I felt that my approach to strategy had evolved substantially from that set out in the original book. The field has moved on, and new theories and perspectives have emerged, notably the "resource-based" approach to competitive strategy. As a consequence, some well-loved techniques, like SWOT analysis, and some popular theories like Michael Porter's "Generic Strategies" have been excluded from this book, because I believe there are better ways to structure analysis, and there are more reliable theories to base prescriptions upon. What has emerged bears little resemblance to the first book in terms of content, but the style and rationale are the same.

Strategy in Practice focuses on the challenges faced by managers who have to contribute to strategy debates within their firms. It aims to provide a structured approach to "strategizing", through a combination of proven practical techniques and relevant theory. Each chapter concludes with a "So what?" question, which explores the practical implications of the material in the chapter. Posing this question has been valuable, and some material has been eliminated from earlier drafts that could not pass this test. I have included illustrations culled from newspapers to help the reader link theory to practice, and a brief case study at the end of the book can be used as a context to explore and debate some of the techniques and arguments set out.

I would like to thank my colleagues Mark Jenkins and Simon Carter for their ideas and insights that have informed the discussion of strategy processes. I would also like to thank Veronique Ambrosini for her contributions to the book as a whole, and specifically for her help in the sections dealing with resource-based theory and tacit knowledge. I would like to thank Elaine Parocki for her help in putting the whole thing together in her usual supportive, patient and efficient manner. Thanks Elaine! Finally I would like to thank Christine for her support and encouragement throughout this project.

CHAPTER 1

A sense of strategy

Introduction

A sense of strategy is an important component in the management of a successful business. By a sense of strategy I mean that the top management team have a shared understanding of where the firm is trying to go. Some view of where and how the firm is trying to compete gives confidence to managers from the top downwards. It assists managers in making resourcing decisions, and it can instil a sense of purpose. But because the future is uncertain it is impossible to rationally analyze the firm's situation in a way which produces a single "correct" strategy for the business. However, faced with uncertainty and complexity, *some* sense of direction is better than *no* sense of direction. We can take heart from the fact that a "right answer" is not attainable. A-well-thought-through and well-argued strategy will not necessarily be the "optimal" strategy for the business, and there may be several viable alternatives, each with their advantages and disadvantages. Nevertheless, a shared and agreed view of where we are trying to take the firm is an essential ingredient for the successful management of *today's* activities. Armed with this shared understanding, managing on a day-to-day basis becomes more straightforward. If we know where we are trying to head, difficult operational and resourcing decisions can be made with more confidence.

But setting the strategic direction for a business is the most complex task facing any top management team. The complexity arises for a variety of reasons that are peculiar to strategy making, as follows:

- strategy is about an unknown future;
- there are many paths that a firm could follow; and
- firms operate in dynamic competitive environments.

Because strategy making involves people, however, the complexity is compounded:

◆ each executive involved has his or her own views and motives, which may or may not be explicit; and

◆ in deciding strategy, individuals are constrained by their past experiences, taken-for-granted assumptions, biases and prejudices.

There are ways of dealing with these layers of complexity. One is to avoid the problem of strategy altogether by running the business on an ad hoc basis. This can work as long as the things the firm is doing continue to be relevant to the markets it operates within. Sadly, recent history is littered with examples of firms that were market leaders in the 1980s, but which have hit the rocks in the 1990s.

Many firms have tried to deal with an uncertain future through planning systems. At the simpler end of the spectrum, these are merely extended budgeting processes, and at the more elaborate end they are characterized by extensive phases of analysis, option generation and evaluation, leading through to detailed implementation planning. Planning systems, though, have come in for a good deal of justifiable criticism. Many senior executives would recognize them as a corporate ritual, largely driven by unrealistic performance targets, and which rarely feed through to implementation.

Unfortunately, this experience of planning has coloured many executives' opinions about strategy. This book is about strategy, not planning. It is designed to help managers who are seriously trying to debate their firm's strategy. The emphasis is on trying to answer some fundamental questions about the firm's future direction. And in addressing these questions, some analytical techniques and frameworks are explained. The stress, however, is clearly on the quality of the strategy *debate*, and not on a numbers-driven budgeting exercise, underpinned by the spurious accuracy that only spreadsheet projections can provide.

Once a shared understanding about these questions has been arrived at, then more detailed action planning can take place to try to turn the broad intentions into understandable tasks that need to be tackled today. Clearly, at this point in the development of strategy, targets and budgets will need to be set to help in the implementation of the strategy.

Senior managers have to make strategic decisions. They are not in the comfortable position of an academic observer, who, while being able to point out how complex everything is, can always walk away from the problem. The essence of senior management work is to wrestle with the problems of strategy. This book is therefore for people who have to become involved in setting the strategic direction for their company. The concepts, models and techniques explained should be regarded as "tools for thought". None of them give the right answer to the strategy problem. They are designed to help executives *structure* a strategy debate; they do not take the place of that debate!

All the tools explained in this book have been used and developed with top teams. The tools help focus and structure debates in helpful ways. Benefits are derived from the thinking and discussion involved in applying the tools, as well as from the insights generated through the analysis. None of the techniques is a substitute for the exercise of judgement. The techniques covered force important questions to be asked which are not routinely discussed. This prompts a search for better information, for example, on customers' real needs, and it usually provokes a more critical evaluation of the assumptions we make about the firm, its customers and competitors. So these tools also help us to surface some of these assumptions, which then enables us to challenge them.

Levels of strategy

It is important to distinguish three levels of strategy: corporate; business; and operational or functional. These three levels are set out in the form of an organizational structure in Figure 1.1. We have to be clear, when debating strategy, which level we are talking about. If this is not clear, it is very easy to become confused in the discussions.

Corporate strategy

A corporation is typically a large organization divided into a number of discrete and fairly autonomous units or divisions ("strategic business units" or SBUs). Setting corporate strategy is the responsibility of the

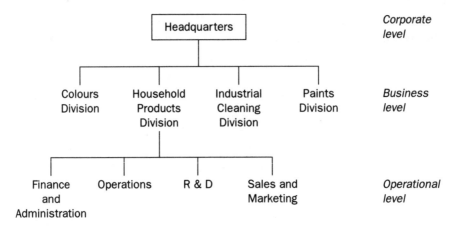

Figure 1.1 *Levels of strategy*

corporate headquarters. The fundamental issue at the corporate level is the *logic* or rationale for the corporation. In other words, why have these different businesses been collected together under one corporate roof?

Various arguments have been put forward to answer this question. These include the *synergy* argument, that by combining these particular businesses the whole will perform better than the sum of the individual parts (2 + 2 = 5). These potential benefits would include scale economies, sharing core competences, cross-selling, and leveraging a strong brand image across a variety of product groups.

Another rationale is the "holding company" or portfolio management logic. Here, advantage is to be gained by grouping diverse businesses together, for instance to smooth out profit streams, or to benefit from the more efficient allocation of capital between different businesses. Other corporations have been built on the back of the financial or "turnaround" expertise of corporate management. But the critical issue is that there must be a logic, and this reason or rationale for grouping different businesses together must inform the way in which these businesses are managed from the corporate centre. A holding company logic would require a fairly "hands-off" remote role for the corporate centre, whereas a "core competence" logic would suggest more involvement from the centre in fostering the leveraging of competences from one SBU into another.

Business strategy

The critical issue at the level of an individual business or SBU is *competitive strategy*. This can be tackled by addressing the following five questions:

1. *What markets should we be trying to compete in?* What segments of those markets should we be clearly focusing on?

2. *How should we try to compete in those segments?* How do we think we can gain and sustain a competitive advantage?

3. *What key competences do we need to build to realize this competitive strategy?* And how should we organize the business?

4. *What do we look like now?* That is, in relation to what we need to look like in order to successfully implement this strategy?

5. *How can we move forward?*

These key questions underpin the structure of this book, and the tools and techniques set out in the following chapters are designed to help a team to debate these questions.

Operational strategy

Operational strategies are, for example, marketing strategies, manufacturing strategies, quality assurance, information systems and finance strategies. Most firms have some sort of functional structure where, in order to gain the benefits of specialization, people focus on a subset of the overall tasks of the firm. Logically, the business-level strategy is implemented through the appropriate operational- or functional-level strategies. So the overall business strategy has to be translated into a linked set of operational-level strategies.

However, in practice, this connection between business and functional strategies is not straightforward. Many actions that are required to implement the chosen business strategy might not be routinely picked up by the existing structure; these actions either fall between existing responsibilities, or they cut right across the organization. Moreover, the broad strategic intentions set out in the business-level strategy can often be watered down as it passes to functional or operational levels. A key problem in implementation is that each functional area may interpret the business strategy in a way that suits itself. This may be done quite unconsciously, as functional managers may be more comfortable in dealing with the aspects of the strategy that fit their personal past experiences. We shall return to this issue in Chapter 7.

Strategy processes

The strategy process is the way in which the strategy was arrived at or decided. How the strategy comes about critically affects the chances of successful implementation. Strategy processes affect the *quality of the strategy* that emerges from the process, and the level to which the top team of the firm are *committed* to the strategy.

Clearly, there is little point in having a high-quality strategy that no one is committed to implementing, and similarly it would be dangerous to have a high level of commitment to a poor strategy. In Figure 1.2 we take these two dimensions, quality and commitment, and set out four different types of strategy process outcomes: impoverished, consultant's, blinkered and required.

Impoverished strategy

Here, the strategy emerging from the process is poor and (perhaps fortunately!) there are low levels of top-team commitment to it. Most

Commitment to strategy

	Lo	Hi
Hi	Consultant's strategy 2	Required strategy 4
Lo	Impoverished strategy 1	Blinkered strategy 3

Quality of strategy

Figure 1.2 *Strategy process outcomes*

"mission statements" can be located in this cell, particularly if they contain pious platitudes that no one really believes. Unfortunately, mission statements have been devalued as a strategy device because they have been used indiscriminately and have been thrust into organizations in inappropriate ways. In some respects, a mission statement has become a fashion item ("everyone else has one, so perhaps we should have one too"). This is unfortunate because a well-crafted mission statement can be a powerful working document. But it must be preceded by a thorough analysis of the organization's situation, which seeks to answer the five basic questions set out above. Thus the strategy needs to be thought through first. Then, if the essence of the strategy can be captured in a concise statement of intent, the mission statement means something.

We could include a great deal of business planning in this impoverished cell. For many businesses, planning is a tedious ritual that rarely leads to significant improvements in strategy. A typical planning process might begin with the HQ planning staff sending out an edict requiring subsidiary units to submit their plans for the next four years by 1 September. There may be some guidelines about the format that should be used in compiling the plans and budgets. This request may be greeted with a certain lack of enthusiasm at the business-unit level, but they comply with it and submit their plans. These plans may well be rejected by HQ (often for being insufficiently ambitious, and for not planning to meet the performance targets set by group HQ), and a redrafting of the plan requested. The business-unit managers conclude that "if they want different numbers, then let's give them different numbers!" The process drifts further away from reality with each iteration, leading to an outcome that is entirely unsatisfactory.

The net result of such a process is that the business-level managers will probably do what they intended to do anyway, which may bear very little relationship to the final version of their plan. This is partly because the business-level managers do not "own" the plan. If they feel that overambitious targets have been set by corporate HQ, then the plans to achieve those targets have a sense of unreality about them. What happens to the plans at corporate HQ? Not a great deal, usually; they may be aggregated in some way, and they will certainly be filed somewhere.

In this rather jaundiced account of some planning processes it is worth considering why people at senior levels in a corporation are engaging in what amounts to a rather sterile ritual. One possible explanation is that corporate staff feel they are not sufficiently in control of events at the business-unit level. One way of exercising some influence is by engaging in the planning process, although if this is ineffective, all that is being achieved is an *illusion* of control.

Finally, there can be a problem of "strategy overload" in some businesses. In such cases, the organization has a vision statement, a statement of core values, strategic objectives, a total quality policy, equal opportunities and environmental awareness policies, and more. The profusion of strategy statements leads to confusion and often cynicism. There are too many important and critical objectives. Staff may derive some cynical satisfaction from pointing out inconsistencies between these various statements of strategic intent.

Consultant's strategy

In this cell there is high-quality strategy but low levels of top-team commitment to it. The strategy may well have been produced by outside consultants, but the same effect can result when a planning or business development department is seen to be the major contributor to the strategy. The quality of the strategy should be good, because the consultants are experienced in analysis and strategy formulation, and they can be more objective. The key problem here is the lack of ownership of the strategy by members of the top team, provoking a "not invented here" attitude. Typical responses from individual members of the top team on being confronted with the strategy include the following:

- ◆ *Selective approval* You find something in the report that agrees with what you have been arguing in the past, and use it to bolster your case.

- ◆ *Undermining the report's credibility* This is achieved by pointing out errors of detail in the report.

- ◆ *Postponement* "I like the strategy but now is not the time to implement it."

- ◆ *Overt rejection* "The consultants don't understand our business."

This lack of ownership can also be manifested when the top team itself is heavily involved in deciding the strategy. A subtle distancing process may take place when team members realize that in order to implement the strategy they personally will have to change what they do. This can cause anxiety, as it can move the team member away from his or her past successful experiences. A lack of commitment can manifest itself in comments such as, ''We like the strategy, but we know that corporate HQ won't support it, so it is not our fault if it is not implemented.''

Some strategy and planning processes can be viewed by top-team participants as merely exercises, rather than a real, deliberate intention to shape the future direction of the business. It is almost as if the team were discussing someone else's organization, or even a business-school case study. Little feeling or emotion is generated in these rather sterile debates.

Blinkered strategy

In this cell we have a poor-quality strategy, but the team is strongly committed to it. This outcome emerges when the strategy debate is heavily constrained by the limited past experiences of the team. Typically, if the team consists of people who have spent most of their careers either in the same firm or within the same industry, they are likely to have problems in deriving novel strategies. These same past experiences can severely restrict the breadth of the discussion. They will probably restrict their discussions to incremental adjustments to the existing strategy. We shall explore the blinkered strategy further with the use of Figure 1.3.

The zone of comfortable debate

The debate can be further limited where critical but uncomfortable issues are avoided. Figure 1.3 suggests three zones of debate. The outer zone, the zone of comfortable debate, is one in which the team can operate quite happily. As long as the discussions stay within the acceptable boundaries of incremental change, team members feel all right. Or team members can remain comfortable if the strategy process is assumed to be an ''unreal'' event. For instance, based on past experience, nothing happens anyway, so we feel free to suggest ambitious strategies. But unless the team enters the zone of uncomfortable debate, little real progress is likely to be made.

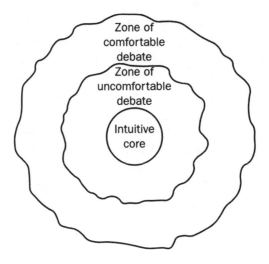

Figure 1.3 *Zones of strategy debate*

The zone of uncomfortable debate

People know when they are entering the zone of uncomfortable debate
– tension is heightened, and a typical response is to defuse the tension
so that the team can slide back into the comfortable zone. Issues that
can be found lurking in the zone of uncomfortable debate include the
following:

◆ Relationships between team members (A hates B).

◆ Realistic assessments of competence.

◆ The style of the chief executive officer.

◆ Challenging sacred cows (i.e. accepted theories and practices).

If these issues are real and important, unless they are addressed the
strategy debate will be largely a bogus exercise. Often it is not even that
individuals are unaware of these problems, but simply that they are
never brought up in formal discussion. So they lurk underneath, yet
they can still strongly influence the surface level of the debate. For
example, animosity between the chief executive officer and another
director is expressed through the chief executive shooting down ideas
and suggestions that are thought to emanate from the other director's
department. If some of these issues are not dealt with, a false strategy
will be adopted. Team members will overtly agree with it, but they
probably have no intention of implementing it.

The intuitive core

The intuitive core refers to a set of beliefs and assumptions held in common by the team and taken for granted. It can include assumptions about what customers want, who the competitors are, what the real strengths are, and so on. The problem lies in the fact that the assumptions remain implicit. If these assumptions are not brought into the open, they cannot be challenged or debated. The more experiences the team members have in common, the more likely they are to share these assumptions, which has the effect of severely constraining the scope of the debate.

The intuitive core acts like a filter or lens that is used by managers to interpret or make sense of the world. "Facts" don't speak for themselves: they are interpreted on the basis of the manager's past experience. If team members share common experiences they are likely to find it very difficult to conceive of strategies that move them away significantly from the current modi operandi in the organization.

Part of the purpose of using the strategy techniques and concepts explained in this book is to help a team to broaden out the debate by probing assumptions held in the team's intuitive core. For example, in assessing the competitive environment (using tools explained in Chapter 5), key assumptions will be challenged, such as, "Who are we really competing with?" Similarly, assumptions about customer needs will surface and hence can be questioned (see Chapter 2).

Regrettably, for some team members the great attraction of a strategy process that ends up as "impoverished", "consultant's" or "blinkered" is that they personally do not have to change what they do. Each of these three outcomes results in minimal adjustments to the status quo.

Required strategy

The ideal process is where high levels of commitment are generated around a good-quality strategy. How, then, can the team members ensure that they will achieve this outcome (assuming of course that this is what they want to achieve)? The following guidelines can help a team to end up in the required strategy cell:

◆ The team members should debate strategy among themselves, and not rely on outsiders to formulate the strategy.

- However, they must be prepared to enter the zone of uncomfortable debate, and attempt to lay open and challenge their taken-for-granted assumptions.

- They may find that an outside facilitator can help them in this process. Note, though, that the consultant is a *facilitator*, not a decider of strategy.

- The debate will not happen during routine management meetings. Time must therefore be set aside for these discussions.

- Expect the process to take time. Time is needed to gather the right sort of information for a strategic analysis, and it takes time to convince ourselves (and others) of the need for change.

- Use some of the tools and frameworks set out in this book to help structure the debate: these aids will help the team to raise critical questions; they can focus the discussion; and they can provide a common language.

- Rotate a "devil's advocate" role around the group. The devil's advocate's job is to challenge and criticize assumptions, beliefs and decisions.

- Always allow yourselves a cooling off period so that decisions made can be scrutinized later in the cold light of reality!

- Obtain better information on competitors and customers.

- Try to summarize the emerging strategy in a concise statement of intent. This statement should be a live, internal management document, not a PR statement.

- Translate the broad strategy into a set of actions. Each action should be owned by one individual, who will feel accountable for its implementation.

- Monitor progress through routine meetings that are set aside specifically for strategy review.

Confidence in setting strategy

As I asserted at the start of the chapter, there are no "right answers" in strategy. I believe that if a team can unite behind a broad understanding of where they think the business should be going, they can gain in confidence. This shared sense of direction helps members of the executive team to make important operational decisions. The feeling of direction cascades down the structure, and this will help to increase confidence among middle-level managers.

It is the responsibility of senior executives to set the strategic direction for their business or business unit. Some find the task too difficult, and spend most of their time engaging in important operational or functional work. This reluctance to engage in the strategic agenda is understandable. If you have no training in strategy, you have to make your contribution in the areas of the business where you feel you have expertise. This is invariably within the functional area in which you have built your career. But the strategic implications of this understandable behaviour are serious. The most predictable outcome is "strategic drift", where, through small incremental adjustments to the status quo, the firm drifts further away from the more rapidly changing environment. This eventually precipitates a crisis, as the mismatch between what the firm is doing and the changed business environment results in a serious downturn in performance.

Often the crisis acts as a trigger for change, forcing the management team to act dramatically. Unfortunately, the easiest reaction to a serious downturn in performance is to cut costs. This rarely leads through to a sustainable competitive position. In this rather negative way, however, at least the top management are forced to behave strategically ("There is no alternative").

The confidence to drive through strategic change can also result from past experiences of successfully effecting such change, or from personal experience of the successful "solution". This is why major change often only occurs when a new CEO is introduced into the firm. This individual can confidently apply a well-understood "recipe" learned through personal experience from another organization. So the new CEO is parachuted in to a new (for him) context with an "old" (for him) solution. He knows it works, so he can drive the changes through in the new context. Illustration 1.1 explains some problems Ann Iverson was facing as CEO of Laura Ashley. It is worth thinking about where her confidence to act boldly stemmed from. Was it from her years of personal experience of retailing, or was it, more specifically, her involvement with successful turnarounds at Mothercare and BHS? And in setting a new direction for Laura Ashley, did her confidence in her vision derive from a

1.1 Is it curtains for Ann Iverson?

Ann Iverson took on a tough task when she accepted the top job at Laura Ashley: to restore the fading fortunes of a company bogged down in outdated floral flocks, chintz curtains and taffeta ballgowns. Her reward was a multimillion pound pay deal that had her branded the first female fat cat.

That was two years ago. And until just two months ago, everything was going to plan for the 53 year old from Michigan, USA. Profits were up, the store group was growing and the share price had improved.

Then, in one day, it all started to go wrong. On April 24, Iverson was forced to admit that the group had bought too much stock and had not opened enough new stores to sell it – a basic error for a retailer. It was a £4m. mistake, but because the City cannot cope with shocks, it wiped £100m. off the company's value.

The bad news didn't end there. Two of Iverson's hand-picked deputies quit simultaneously, amid rumours of acrimony; then it emerged that her pay packet had been revised, *upwards*, so that she banked a cool £1.1m. last year. City shareholders don't mind fat pay packets, but when a big rise comes hot on the heels of bad news, they see red – and ask awkward questions about management style. Where Iverson is concerned, there's plenty to talk about. She has a fearsome reputation. She admits she is aggressive, confrontational and "brutally frank", and says she takes "personal responsibility" for every aspect of the business. To some, that means a hands-on approach; to others, it means she interferes in everything.

Born in Michigan, daughter of a factory manager, Iverson was educated privately in Denver. When she was 16, her family moved to the West Coast, where she caught "the retail bug": she took an after-school job behind a department store counter. It was "absolutely fabulous".

She went off to university with the aim of becoming a teacher, but dropped out before qualifying, got married, had a son, separated, and soon ended up back behind that same counter. But it wasn't just a dead-end job for a single mother: she worked her way through the retailing ranks, eventually joining Bloomingdales, before being head-hunted by department store Bonwit Teller.

When David Dworkin, the Bonwit Teller boss, was recruited to head Storehouse in the UK – the Habitat, Mothercare and Bhs empire built up by Sir Terence Conran – he brought Ann Iverson with him as his deputy. She won praise for turning around Mothercare and Bhs. But when Dworkin returned to the US in 1993, she headed home, too, as boss of toy-store chain Kay-Bee.

It was back in America that she was introduced, by a merchant banker, to Sir Bernard Ashley, who founded Laura Ashley with his wife in the 1950s. He promptly hired her to work her magic on his ailing company. It certainly was ailing. The company had been a 1970s and 1980s icon – but it has lost its way, both in fashion and in finance.

Iverson was appointed chief executive in 1995 – the fourth boss since 1990. The £16m. profit she turned in last year was the company's best result since 1989. The recovery has been based on completely revamping the Laura Ashley image. The twee floral patterns and leg-of-mutton ballgowns have been ditched in favour of elegant modern classics. Where the flowers remain, they are black and white or bold rose designs. The interior design range has also been updated and expanded. Iverson's plan is for an upmarket label that can compete with the likes of Ralph Lauren.

Her US ad campaign carried the slogan: "Laura Ashley – say it without flowers". It is a risky business strategy, which threatens alienating existing customers before finding new ones. One middle-aged British shareholder said it all when he told Iverson at the company's recent annual meeting that his wife, in her mid-fifties and a lifelong Laura Ashley shopper, couldn't find anything suitable in the stores any more. Iverson's response was that she hoped his wife could, but that the shops had been refocused to target 35 year olds.

The new focus mirrors her own image. She shuns the power-dressed executive suit and favours casual elegance, from well-cut trousers and flat shoes to flowing jersey two-pieces with high, strappy sandals. Her trademark is jewellery: multiple bangles, dangling earrings and even a ring on her thumb. Her nails and lips are always polished, her straight blonde hair cut in a simple, no-fuss style.

The changes Iverson set in motion didn't stop in the shops: she moved head office from Maidenhead to Chelsea Harbour – just a short stroll from her home – and replaced most of the shop executives with her own choices. In came six women to ten of the most senior positions, though she insists she hires on merit, not gender.

She oozes charm – and all the evidence of being a control freak. It is her strategy, her plan, her responsibility, her decision. In a recent BBC documentary, she publicly humiliated a member of her staff over a trifling detail. Although the company denies it, her senior colleagues were said to be furious. She claims she is not ruthless, but admits to making quick decisions and acting on them swiftly, whether it's a detail about displaying merchandise or firing a member of staff. She doesn't, she says, "expect others to keep up with me".

She is a workaholic: she labours six days a week, often 14 hours a day. She rarely takes holidays and claims to have no hobbies. Sunday is her day of rest, when she sometimes sleeps for 20 hours, but always goes to church. She believes in God and says it is this belief that gives her strength.

In the coming months, she is going to need every bit of that strength. When you are succeeding, tough attributes are viewed as winning ways. When you are being battered, they are seen as dictatorial. And dictators are always in danger of being deposed.

Last weekend, it was reported that shareholders have given her four months to produce the goods – and sell them. Her plan, her decisions, must work, and fast. Ann Iverson cannot afford another mistake.

(Source: *Guardian*, Tuesday, 10 June 1997.)

personal identification with the outlook and values of the new target customer: that is, was she, in effect, selling to herself?

We cannot rely either on crisis or on some miracle worker dropping into the organization with a ready-made solution to solve the strategic issues facing our organzation. The top team of the firm need to develop confidence and genuine belief in a strategy themselves. This is not easy. However, where a top team can confidently tackle the strategic agenda and can set a strategic direction for the organization, this can almost visibly "empower" them, giving them confidence to behave in more definite and focused ways. This does not, of course, solve the problem of energizing and motivating the management levels below the top team (we take this issue up later in the book). Nevertheless, one thing is certain: the first priority must be to unite the top team around a shared sense of direction for the business. This is a prerequisite for tackling the rest of the organization.

The plan of the book

The book is structured around the key questions set out earlier. However, although logically we should consider addressing the market environment first, for process reasons which are explained later, I choose to enter the debate by initially exploring the nature of competitive advantage. Thus the structure is as follows:

◆ *How should we try to compete?* How do we think we can gain and sustain a competitive advantage? These issues are explored in Chapter 2.

◆ *What key competences do we need to build to realize this competitive strategy?* This question is addressed in Chapter 3.

◆ *What markets should we be trying to compete in?* What segments of those markets should we clearly be focusing on? Techniques to explore these questions are explained in Chapter 4.

◆ *How should we organize the business?* This is the concern of Chapter 5.

◆ *What do we look like now?* That is, in relation to what we need to look like to successfully implement this strategy? Ways of examining the culture of the organization are explained in Chapter 6.

◆ *How can we move forward?* Chapter 7 explores the problems of managing strategic change, and provides some guidelines on successful change practices.

◆ Finally, Chapter 8 is concerned with strategy at the *corporate* level.

The techniques and tools explained in this book require good information: in particular, on customers and competitors. The techniques cannot take the place of creativity and judgement, but they can provide a focus for debate, and they can force issues on to the agenda which are often ignored. No matter how much information is gathered, and no matter how well it is marshalled in analysis and argument, at the end of the day the team will only agree with what they believe should be done. Some of this belief derives from intuition or "gut feel", some from more objective analysis and discussion. The tools can be used with imperfect information: what is important is the debate that ensues, not the precision of the data that can be realistically gathered. This process is not "science", and there is a strong requirement for intuition and creativity, which can hopefully be encouraged through the challenging questions raised by the techniques. Strategy-making is not a precise procedure that can be reduced to a set of rational tools, and although the analyses might lack rigour and precision, my question to you would be: "What strategy process is *currently* being employed in your organization?" In other words, what is this replacing?

So what?

Since this is supposed to be a practical book, at the end of each chapter I have included a "So what?" section. The purpose of this section is to force us to address, from an executive's point of view, the practical implications of the material in the chapter. This is a good discipline for an academic like me, and it is the question that many managers ask about much of what we academics like to write. I subscribe to the view that we need to understand the complex realities of strategy before we can start to draw up prescriptions about what practising managers can do to be more strategically effective. There is, nevertheless, a worrying divide in the field. On the one hand, we have writers, who could best be described as consultants, who are almost solely concerned with practice. And on the other hand, we have academics who are primarily driven by the need to publish in academic journals, and who are not in the least concerned whether their contributions have any practical relevance. Neither extreme is acceptable.

The "theory free" consultant is only able to proffer shallow prescriptions which do not stand up to rigorous scrutiny. The prescriptions come and go almost as fashion items (remember "management by objectives", corporate planning, quality circles, "in search of excellence"?). The academic, concerned only with being recognized by his peers cannot engage meaningfully with practising managers. The theory they generate can be sterile, and hedged around with so many restrictive assumptions that it makes no sense to those engaging with the complexities of the real world.

But we all need theory! Theories are beliefs concerning how we think the world works. If you consider that the way to improve sales figures is to push more sales people out on to the streets, then you have a belief about the cause-and-effect relationship between sales effort and sales results. These "theories in use" have usually been developed from experience, and they may well be very well founded. The contribution that academics can make is to take a more structured and rigorous approach to the development of theory. If it is good theory it will probably lead to good practice.

The "So what?" section is therefore an attempt to clearly link the largely conceptual material in the chapters to the practical agenda of an executive who has some responsibility for the strategy of the organization. Thus the "So what?" points derived from this chapter are as follows:

- Strategy is a shared understanding of where we are taking the organization.

- A sense of strategy can give confidence to the members of a top team, and it can help them to make difficult decisions.

- There are no "right answers", but some sense of strategy is better than no sense of strategy. This should be a liberating thought, encouraging you to engage with the strategic agenda.

- Strategy is complicated, so you need some straightforward questions to guide you through the process.

- Be very clear about the distinction between corporate, business and functional level strategy.

- Analytical techniques do not provide answers, but they can help to structure your discussions. They raise important questions that are not routinely asked, and they can help to uncover assumptions we may share.

- You will only really believe in a strategy that you have created. Ownership of the strategy comes from genuine involvement in the strategy-making process.

- A *real* strategy debate can be difficult and challenging – so be prepared to enter the zone of uncomfortable debate.

At the end of the book I have included a brief case study, S. J. Matthews. You can use this case in the following way. If you read it now, before you embark on the rest of the book, you can familiarize yourself with the situation of this small firm. Then, when you read each chapter, think about the kinds of *questions* you would ask about this firm and its situation, based on the issues raised in the chapter. There are, of course, no "right answers", but being able to operate effectively at a strategic level requires skill in knowing what sort of questions to pose. This then guides your search for more information, and it focuses and structures the ensuing strategy debate.

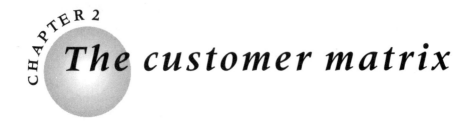

CHAPTER 2

The customer matrix

Introduction

In Chapter 1 we explained the difference between corporate-level strategy and business-level strategy. The critical strategic question at business level is how can the business gain and sustain competitive advantage? A great deal has been written on this subject, notably by Michael Porter. His "Generic Strategy" concepts have proved to be popular, providing a straightforward choice to managers between cost leadership and differentiation strategies. More recently, Hamel and Prahalad's work on core competences has been influential in shifting the focus of attention to the internal capabilities of the organization. This work has been supported by parallel developments of a more theoretical nature, referred to as the "resource-based" theory of the firm. In this and the following two chapters a different approach is developed that builds on these foundations, but which also has a very practical element. These three chapters explore arguments about competitive strategy, and, in addition, introduce practical tools that can be used to analyze the competitive situation of any business. For a fuller account of this approach the reader should refer to Bowman and Faulkner's *Competitive and Corporate Strategy* (Irwin, 1997).

The customer matrix

This chapter introduces the *customer matrix*, a helpful device that can be used to explore competitive strategy. This matrix is derived from the perceptions that customers have of the products/services being offered to them, and the prices that they are being charged. On the vertical axis of Figure 2.1, the *perceived use value* (PUV) refers to the value perceived

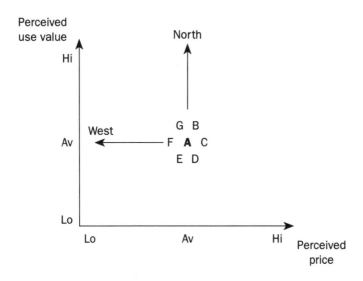

Figure 2.1 *Two basic strategies for the customer matrix*

by the buyer in purchasing and using the product or the service; the horizontal axis is the *perceived price* (PP). Perceived use value and perceived price represent the two components of "value for money", and the customer matrix separates out these components to assist us in analyzing competitive strategy. Perceived price refers to the elements of price that the customer is concerned with. For example, in purchasing a heating system for a house the customer may not only be concerned with the initial cost of the installation (the price of the boiler, radiators, fitting, etc.), but may also be interested in the running costs of the system over the years (fuel costs, maintenance, etc.).

A customer matrix can only be derived from the perceptions of a single individual. We would all have slightly different perceptions of the same collection of, say, family cars. What we would be looking for in terms of perceived use value, or utility, from the purchase of a car would differ from one customer to the next. What elements of price we pay attention to would also vary. For example, one customer might regard insurance and running costs as a vital cost element, whereas another customer would be more concerned with initial purchase price, and the likely rate of depreciation over two years of ownership. Similarly, how we individually assess alternative products will vary. In trying to understand customer behaviour, therefore, we must be prepared to recognize that there may be important differences between potential customers. People don't all see things the same way.

Segments of demand

In order to develop a customer matrix it is necessary to identify a discrete segment of demand: that is, a group of potential customers who share similar needs and have similar perceptions of use value. A segment thus defined might include a quite disparate collection of people. What they share in common is, first, a set of preferences, and second, a set of similar perceptions of what use values meet those underlying preferences.

When trying to construct a customer matrix it can be helpful to have in mind a particular individual who might fairly well represent a segment of demand. This reduces the risks of making inappropriate generalizations. If there are wide variations in needs we may conclude that the market should be further segmented. Within a segment, however, there may still be differing perceptions of a product's relative position, due to differences both in weightings of dimensions of PUV, and in perceptions of a product's attributes. At the end of the chapter we shall examine how a matrix can be constructed; for now, we shall use the customer matrix to help us explore some issues in competitive strategy.

Representing products on the matrix

In order to develop an argument about competitive strategy, we shall show the positions of products only from the perspective of the "average" customer in a segment. In Figure 2.1 the letters A–G represent the positions of products in the matrix. In other words, a representative or "average" customer in this segment would perceive the products on offer to be grouped in this way. As far as this average customer is concerned, all the firms are offering more or less equivalent products and are charging very similar prices. So, as far as this representative customer is concerned, there is no real difference between the products on offer. This situation can be found in many industries, and not just in those that are supplying obvious "commodity" products like gasoline or potatoes. In any circumstance where consumers perceive the products or services on offer to be more or less the same, the industry approximates to the circumstances depicted in Figure 2.1. This could be the case in, for example, the personal computer hardware market, or in the choice of estate agents.

If the firm with product A is facing the situation depicted in Figure 2.1, what are the options available for improving its competitive position? As things now stand in this industry it is likely that all the firms will have a similar share of the market, so how can this firm (product A) improve its share? There are various moves that could be made in the chart which could improve the firm's competitive position. For example, the firm could cut price by moving westward in the matrix, or it could raise the perceived use value of the products or services it offers (moving northwards), or indeed do both at the same time. These two basic strategy options will now be explored.

Cutting price

Here the firm moves *west* in the customer matrix, offering the same perceived use value as the competition, but at a lower price (see Figure 2.1). Such a move should lead to Firm A gaining share. However, this may depend on the type of products or services being offered, and on the likely reaction of competitors. In some markets, buyers perceive lower price to mean lower perceived use value. In other words, price is being used as an indirect way of measuring use value, where the customer reasons that, "If it's cheaper, it can't be as good as the others." If this was the situation facing Firm A, then a cut in price would move the firm to the *south-west*, to a position offering lower perceived use value at lower prices. The price cut might therefore lead to a disappointing result, where the expected sales increases did not materialize. Managers have to be alert to this possibility. It often occurs where customers are unfamiliar with the purchase situation, and they seek to reduce the riskiness of the purchase by using price as a proxy for value (e.g. when buying wine, dishwashers, cars, consultancy).

Let us assume that consumers are *not* using price as a proxy measure of perceived use value, and that the price cut moves Firm A due west on the chart. This move should increase sales for Firm A, and maybe in the industry as a whole, if new consumers are attracted into the market by the lower prices. However, other firms are likely to respond to the move by cutting prices to match Firm A in order to preserve their share of the market – they may even undercut Firm A. Thus the net result of the competitors moving west with Firm A is to reduce average price and profitability in the industry.

Competitors can, then, imitate Firm A's price-cutting strategy very rapidly – overnight if necessary. How, therefore, can Firm A hope to gain an enduring advantage from competing on price? In order to achieve a sustainable advantage, Firm A must be able to continually drive down prices, and to sustain lower prices for a longer period than its competitors. This can only be achieved if Firm A either has the lowest costs in the industry, or is able to sustain losses for extended periods, for example through subsidies from another part of the corporation, or from government sources. If a firm is not the lowest-cost producer, then the competitor that *is* can always cut prices further, or sustain low prices for longer than Firm A. Illustration 2.1 shows how a price-cutting strategy can succeed where the corporation has the resources and resolve to see the strategy through.

Hence, if a firm chooses to compete on price it must have lower costs than its competitors. This requirement involves exploiting all sources of cost reduction that do not affect perceived use value: for example, economies of scale, learning from experience, "right first time" quality, just-in-time manufacturing, and so on. Illustration 2.2 shows that relocating to a lower-cost country can be one way of achieving a more competitive cost position.

Assuming that a firm is able to achieve the lowest-cost position, it could choose to drive out competitors by sustaining very low prices. If, in the course of pursuing this strategy, the firm is able to establish barriers to prevent other firms entering the industry, it could then opt to raise prices – and hence profits – confident of its ability to see off any potential entrants. If it is unable to establish barriers, however, a subsequent rise in price would lead to re-entry by previously defeated competitors, and perhaps by other new entrants.

However, to be sure that the firm is *the* lowest-cost producer it is necessary to be aware of the cost levels of competitors. Without cost information on competitors the management cannot be confident of achieving the lowest-cost position, and unfortunately, this information

2.1 Price wars

Illustration

A price war can only be rewarded if its ultimate result is a change in market behaviour or market structure. Philip Morris, the leading US cigarette manufacturer, achieved both outcomes after initiating a price war in April 1993. The company cut the price of the world's best-selling cigarette – Marlboro – by almost 20 per cent. The immediate effect was to knock almost $10bn dollars off the market value of the company. This surprise move, however, was not perceived by the market as the strategic move it really was – the end of a price war rather than the beginning of one.

Marlboro's share of the US cigarette market had fallen from 30 per cent to 22 per cent, and, in line with other premium cigarette producers, Marlboro had responded to falling volumes of cigarette consumption by pushing up prices in order to maintain profits. Concurrently, manufacturers of generic cigarettes had held down prices to maintain volume. The widening gap between premium and generic products had been filled by low-costs brands, with this segment being led by American Tobacco.

The price war largely destroyed the cheap brands and American Tobacco quit the market altogether by selling the remains of its operations to BAT. The threat of continuing price competition forced the terms of an armistice between the generic manufacturers and premium producers. By 1995 Marlboro had regained its lost market share, and premium and generic prices were drifting up together. The Philip Morris share price more than recovered its lost ground.

Why was the Philip Morris strategy so successful? It succeeded because there were clear objectives and overwhelming commitment on the part of the initiator. Philip Morris's goals were to squeeze the middle segment of the market and to impose price discipline on the generic products, and as one of the world's largest companies it had almost infinite resources which it could mobilize to this end. The competitors were intimidated enough by such muscle to be left in no doubt that Philip Morris would achieve its objectives.

(Source: Adapted by C. Avery from "Mastering management: committed to making a price war pay", *Financial Times*, 5 July 1997.)

is usually difficult to obtain. Indeed, managers in many firms are not at all confident that they understand their *own* cost position, let alone that of their competitors. Nonetheless, it is not impossible to gather intelligence on competitors' costs, although some effort is required, and this issue will be taken up in the next chapter.

Illustration

2.2 A nation of sweatshop keepers

A country like Germany, with its emphasis on systems and innovation, will be dominated by higher-cost companies and must be able to support a well-educated, expensive workforce. Such an economy cannot – by dint of its costs – afford to manufacture low-cost components and products, and will, instead, purchase them from lower-cost, lower-income suppliers who sit further down the industrial value ladder. For the Germans, reaching this economic common sense has been a gradual process which required a marked shift in managerial attitudes, as vertical integration had traditionally been seen as a sound base for wealth creation. Unsurprisingly, the UK has been a beneficiary of this transformation, as many German companies have moved their manufacturing assets into lower-cost countries.

To be fair, the UK does have a number of other attractions: it is a modern country, we speak the international business language, and many Germans are anglophiles. But few people invest in countries simply because they like them, and essentially the Germans are here because it's cheap. If they can extract Bavarian productivity from British workers at British prices, the cost savings are substantial. If this sounds like sweatshop labour for more ambitious, innovative countries, that's because in a way it is. Since its economic heyday, the UK has slipped several rungs down the value ladder. Manufacturing components for German companies may not be the same as sewing T-shirts in the Philippines, but it's not a million miles away either. Moreover, if the UK is to continue to attract even this type of investment, it will have to compete with other countries whose costs – and living standards – are even lower.

Of course, there is always the UK's much-vaunted manufacturing and productivity renaissance, something routinely held up as a shining example of the cure produced by Thatcherism's strong medicine. It is certainly true that the Thatcher years led to a dramatic restructuring of Britain's industrial base. Uncompetitive businesses were allowed to fail, while investment and personal tax incentives encouraged new companies to develop and prosper. Crucially, the trade unions were muzzled and employee rights eroded, allowing the UK to become a more flexible (and arguably less caring) industrial nation, one which could offer attractive business terms to potential investors. Whatever the reasons – a new realism or a fear of the dole queue – it is now beyond dispute that UK industry has become more competitive in international markets.

(Source: *Management Today*, April 1997.)

The risks of competing on price include the following:

◆ The firm may not be able to achieve the lowest costs in the industry. By definition, only one firm can be in this position.

◆ The first firm to compete by cutting prices is likely to provoke its competitors into matching its lower price position as a defensive measure to protect market share. This could lead to a price war, with margins for all but the low-cost players being cut to the bone.

◆ The emphasis on cost-cutting encourages the management to focus inwards on the internal operations of the firm. This may mean that little attention is focused on changing trends, tastes and competitive behaviour in the marketplace.

This last point can lead to a vicious circle for the firm: the inward orientation results in the firm lagging behind changing trends in the marketplace; the firm's products become less competitive, as they have lower perceived use value than the competition; the firm is then forced into competing on price, thus reinforcing the inward, cost-cutting orientation. Ultimately, the firm in this situation may find itself having to offer larger and larger price discounts in order to persuade any consumers to buy its inferior products.

When markets are in decline – either temporarily due to recession, or permanently due to changing customer needs – firms may find themselves forced to compete on price. As we have seen, however, unless a firm has low costs – and preferably the lowest costs – it will inevitably struggle to remain profitable. This would suggest, therefore, that firms should aim to be low cost *whether or not* they intend to compete on price, because market conditions outside their control may force them into price competition.

The firm needs to be low cost compared with those firms which the target customer regards as alternative providers of perceived use value. This may result in quite different definitions of competition from those typically made by managers and industry analysts, and they are likely to encompass fewer rather than many competitors. For example, if you are competing in the specialist sports car market you need to be low cost in relation to other makers of specialist sports cars, not in relation to producers of family cars for the mass market.

Adding perceived use value

The second basic strategy indicated in the customer matrix is the move *north*: gaining advantage through adding more perceived use value for the same price as the competitors' offerings. The starting point for this strategy must be the target customer, and the target customer's perception of value.

In order to effect this move north – rather than achieving it through luck, or trial and error – first, we must be clear who our target customers are. Secondly, we must have a thorough understanding of the target customer's needs, and how that customer evaluates different product offerings.

For example, in choosing a new car the customer – let us assume a male customer in this instance – may have a basic need for flexible transportation. He also has other needs which can be expressed through the car he drives. For instance, meeting his status needs, and his need to belong, may be influential in his selection of a car.

These basic needs are translated into a set of dimensions of use value that are particular to the individual customer. Our status-conscious car buyer requires his car to represent a "lifestyle" to which he aspires, and to deliver good performance, while, at the same time, enabling him to demonstrate his individuality, albeit within the boundaries of acceptability established by his status and need to belong. He is therefore seeking a set of perceived use values that the car must fulfil, and he reasons that if these use values are delivered, his underlying needs will be met. In Figure 2.2 these dimensions of perceived use value are arranged in order of their importance (weightings in brackets) along the horizontal axis. The dimensions of PUV sought are: "classic styling", "performance", "marque strength" (referring to the credibility and acceptability of the brand name), "build quality", and "reliability" (it is important that the car does not break down). The benchmark rating of the strongest competitor in the industry is 5. V, L and M represent different competitive marques of car.

Figure 2.2 indicates that each of these dimensions of PUV is evaluated in some way. The customer uses various criteria to evaluate the extent to which a particular product can deliver a particular dimension of PUV. For example, how is "performance" evaluated? For some customers, acceleration is critical, which may be assessed by inspecting

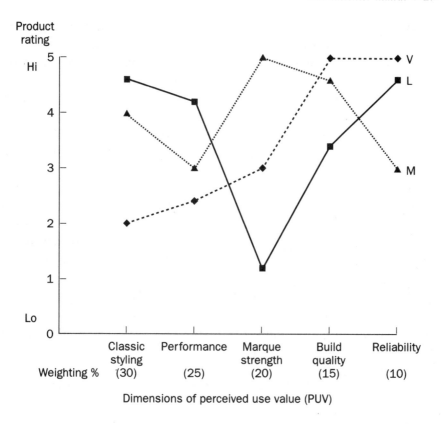

Figure 2.2 *PUV profile: executive cars*

the 0–60 mph statistics; for others, it is top speed that counts. More interestingly, how is "build quality" assessed? The customer may make inferences about build quality by interpreting the sound the car door makes when it is closed. Build quality might also be assessed by inspecting the alignment of body panels, or the paint finish. These may actually be very poor indicators, or poor proxy measures of build quality. However, as customer perceptions are paramount, it is essential that the firm understands what criteria the customer does use in making these evaluations, even if he is "wrong"!

By systematically exploring customer needs and perceptions through market research and by continually listening to customers, firms can discover what is valued in their products and services and what could be added to them to improve perceived use value. Diagrams like the one shown in Figure 2.2 can be constructed to establish the important dimensions of perceived use value for a particular segment.

It appears that one firm's car (product V) is seen to be inferior to the competition on the really important dimensions, but it performs well on the less valued dimensions. If this firm is to move north in the customer matrix, then it has to significantly shift the consumers' perceptions either of its car's performance and styling, through changing the product or maybe by better advertising, or of the dimensions of use value, which would be a more ambitious strategy. For example, it may be possible to persuade some people that reliability is more important than styling. Either way, unless the firm improves its position relative to the competition on these dimensions of perceived use value it will lag behind its competitors. In a below-average position in the customer matrix the firm may find itself forced to cut price to try to preserve sales.

Illustration 2.3 explains how Safeway (UK) tried to refocus its supermarkets to better meet the needs of its target customers. They have identified a segment of demand, and they have tried to understand what these customers value. Having provided this added value to these customers, one of the issues facing Safeway would then be whether competitors like Sainsbury and Tesco could easily copy Safeway and hence destroy their advantage. We explore this issue in more depth in the next chapter.

What happens next?

So the key issue facing firms pursuing a strategy of adding perceived use value is the ease with which competitors can match their moves. As a firm moves north by increasing perceived use value ahead of its competitors, it should be rewarded with an increased share of the market. The duration of this enhanced position will depend on how easily the added perceived use value can be imitated. Over time, it is likely that competitors will be able to imitate the move north, and, as they follow the innovator northwards, the *average* level of perceived use value in the market is ratcheted upwards.

Thus in most industries the minimum acceptable standards are being continuously shifted upwards as competitive moves are imitated: ''order winning'' features become ''order qualifying'' features. For instance,

2.3 **Safeway follows the leader**

Safeway, which has traditionally concentrated on what the marketeers call "early nesters", failed to take account of the dramatic shock to the wallet that having a young family represents, and wasn't providing those young families with the products they wanted at the prices they could afford.

With input from McKinsey, the company devised Safeway 2000, the change programme which was intended not only to propel the retailer over the immediate hurdle, but also to see it over the distance. The first strategic decision was to rule out any attempt to tackle Tesco head on, a wise move.

Safeway 2000 began, logically enough, by identifying the customers who would be key to the company's success. Customer needs – both for products and for services – at every point in their life cycle were identified, and product ranges were modified so that they would be more clearly aimed at families. In concrete terms, this meant less emphasis on the premium parts of key product ranges and more on economy and standard items. One expression of the strategy over the past couple of years has been the rolling out of extremely successful Safeway subbrands (own label products which go out under a different badge), Cyclon in detergents and Vecta in household cleaning products. These have enabled the firm to offer consumers lower price tags while itself benefiting from more than decent margins. At the same time, the company has been able to offer customers price guarantees on around 500 of its most basic lines.

The Safeway store in Camden, north London, which opened just two years ago when the new strategy was really getting under way, shows the extent of the rethink. It has 30 parent-and-child parking spaces near the store entrance, so that parents don't have to fight for a parking space and then drag children (and loaded shopping trolleys) across expanses of tarmac. In the store itself, there is a baby changing room and a crèche which is open from eight in the morning until eight at night.

The Camden store illustrates the progress Safeway has made in other directions too. As part of its customer friendliness, Safeway was the first of the major food multiples to introduce self-scanning, the system it calls Shop & Go. To avoid the usual checkout procedures, this allows loyalty club members to pass their purchases, complete with bar codes, through a hand-held scanner before items are loaded into trolleys or baskets. When shoppers have selected everything they want to buy, the scanner is returned to its dispenser, a bar-coded slip is printed out, and when that is handed in at the pay point, an itemized bill appears. The parallel introduction of what Safeways calls Green

Boxes (cartons customers buy as they enter the store or retain from a previous visit, tessellate into their trolleys, fill up and then unload directly into a car boot) also reduces the hassle. The beauty of the system is that goods don't need to be taken out of the trolley on one side of the checkout simply to be replaced on the other, so the problem of queuing is vastly reduced where it is not eliminated altogether.

(Source: *Management Today*, March 1997.)

anti-lock brakes and air bags are features of cars that were once order winning, but are now essential requirements.

The question of whether or not competitive advantage is sustainable has to be considered against this backdrop of continual northward shifts in the competitive arena. What can the innovator do once the competition have caught up? There are two basic options: keep moving north by staying one jump ahead of the competition through innovation, or move west through a cut in price.

We argued earlier, however, that in order to compete on *price* the firm needs to be the lowest-cost producer in the market. So, can you move north by adding perceived use value, and simultaneously achieve the lowest-cost position? If the move north increases market share, and if these share increases are translated into lower unit costs, through exploiting scale and experience advantages, then there is no reason why the move north could not result in a low relative cost position.

Furthermore, if you *really* understand what it is that customers perceive as value in your products or services, you can confidently strip out everything that does not contribute to that perceived use value. There is no point in offering a range of costly options, if this is not what customers want. Of course, if you are not confident about what customers' needs are and how they evaluate alternative products, then, to play safe, the tendency is to leave everything in the product, because you are not sure which parts of the total package are the valued features.

Illustration 2.4 describes an advertising campaign for Virgin Cola. This campaign highlights how mature markets tend towards commoditized products. In the cola market there are no significant differences in the physical attributes of the products. Differentiation has to be achieved through the development of images or "personalities" for the product. This example also demonstrates that the source of advantage in a maturing product market shifts away from the tangible features of the

2.4 Virgin Cola is being sold on taste – hence the plastic breasts

Enticements to purchase carbonated drinks don't usually begin with a couple of fat men's bottoms. But a new ad for Virgin Cola commences with rumps of this variety wobbling towards a sauna in a forest. Once inside, their owners – a pair of catatonic Finns – flick each other with birch twigs and take slugs of the Branson fizz from a bottle shaped like Pamela Anderson – the "Pammy" – a novelty vessel whose creation marked an earlier attempt to publicize the product. One man sloshes some of his drink on to the hot coals to dramatic effect: he and his companion emerge from the steam to find they are wearing bras and vast plastic breasts.

Carving a niche in the cola market is not easy when the field's two superpowers – Pepsi and Coke – have been flogging their stuff by the millions of gallons since they were (in both cases) invented by entrepreneurial chemists in the American south 100 years ago. But Virgin is investing £5m. trying to do just that. What's needed, it seems, is a whole different profile, something distinctive. So while the giants vie to get closest to that sacred marketing location, "the leading edge", Virgin has entrusted Rainey Kelly Campbell Roalfe with positioning its product in an entirely different part of the consumer's psychological landscape.

It is a place where foreigners are funny and, in most cases, overweight. Hence the flabby Finnish bums. Hence, too, the other three ads in the campaign. One is set in a Turkish prison, where a gigantic tattooed ugly flops on to the top bunk, crushing his terrified cell mate underneath and relieving him of his Virgin Cola can. Another, this for the "diet" version, spoofs a Brazilian television keep-fit show in which a rotund couple dressed in straining Lycra disco dance with road tyres round their middles. Each sips from their can and suddenly – poof! – the tyres disappear.

The last has fun with Italians and the Roman Catholic church. A man visiting a hospital goes to buy a Virgin Cola from a vending machine, but finds his tie pulled in through the cash slot. A passing nun spots his predicament and the fact that the machine has released a can for collection. Reaching between the man's legs, she helps herself to the can and gives a parting pinch to his behind.

The endline, displayed in the form of a movie subtitle, heralds "the unreal world of Virgin Cola", emphasizing a contrast with the glamorized globalism associated with "The Real Thing" and its great rival. It's a sensible approach. In 1986, Pepsi president Roger Enrico wrote that, "taste tests" notwithstanding, "the distinctions between soft drinks are not universally appreciated", and so "imagery is critical to our success". A certain kind of imagery swamps the cola war zone, and a minor protagonist such as Virgin has to stand out from the crowd. Appealing to a "bad taste" aesthetic, rather than proselytizing the pleasant ("good") taste of the drink itself, is a good way to achieve this.

(Source: *Observer Review*, 1 June 1997.)

product, which have long become standard, order-qualifying criteria (like availability, conformance quality), towards more ephemeral, intangible features. This can mean that imitation of the product becomes more, not less difficult, particularly in the case of a brand identity.

Other moves in the customer matrix

If the firm offers higher perceived use value, but demands a price premium for this added value, then this moves the firm's product position to the *north-east* in the matrix (see Figure 2.3). This is Michael Porter's *differentiation* strategy. The success of this strategy depends upon the existence of a group of buyers who are less price sensitive and so are prepared to pay higher prices for the added perceived value. It also

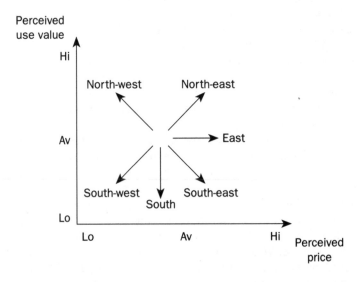

Figure 2.3 *Other competitive moves in the customer matrix*

depends upon the ease with which the added perceived use value can be imitated. If it can readily be imitated by competitors, then the price premium may be rapidly competed away. One other point to note with this move to the north-east is that it may well be shifting the firm's product into a new segment, where customers have different dimensions of use value, and where they may perceive your firm to be competing against different opponents in the market. Moving into this unfamiliar ground can prove to be risky.

The move *east* in Figure 2.3 has the firm increasing price without adding perceived use value. This move can succeed in increasing profitability only if competitors follow suit. In the glass-container industry in Britain in the early 1980s all firms were struggling for profitability; input costs, particularly for gas, were rising and firms did not feel able to pass these costs on to customers. Rockware made a unilateral move to increase prices which was followed by competitors, which resulted in the preservation of relative market shares and increasing profits. If the move is not followed by competitors, then market share will fall.

Moving *south-west* by cutting price *and* perceived use value, is a diagonal move which may well shift the firm into a new market segment. For example, if a car manufacturer located in the middle ground of the car industry (e.g. Ford) took this route it would be moving to a downmarket position. Whereas Ford's competitors might have been GM, Nissan, Renault and Chrysler, it would now find itself being compared by potential customers with Hyundai, Daewoo and Proton. This may be a viable shift as long as the relative cost position of Ford enabled it to operate profitably against these low-price competitors.

The only direction on Figure 2.3 that is guaranteed to deliver an increased share is a move *north-west*, adding value *and* cutting price. The firm must be the lowest-cost producer, and it must be able to move faster than the competitors to sustain its relative position. Typically, however, a competitive firm will initially move north by adding value. Then, when competitors imitate the added value the firm shifts west by cutting price. The share advantage gained through moving north may well enable the firm to become the lowest cost producer through the achievement of scale and experience economies, making the price-cutting strategy feasible. Hence the north-west position is reached by moving north, then west. This is a common strategy used by Japanese companies when they move to attack the global market.

Movements in the customer matrix are determined by changes in customer perceptions of price and perceived use value. Shifts of particular products in the matrix can occur even when the producing firm does nothing. If a competitor is able to move its product north by adding PUV, this has the effect of pushing other competitors' products *south* in the eyes of the customer. Products can be repositioned through changes in customer tastes and preferences, which can alter the dimensions of PUV that are seen to be important by the customer. This may result in products well endowed with the preferred dimensions of PUV moving further north.

In addition to these spontaneous shifts in the customer matrix, as we have argued, firms can obviously seek to reposition their products in the matrix through deliberate acts. However, markets are in a continual state of flux, and the outcomes of actions by one producer will be moderated by actions and reactions of competitors. The linkages between a firm's deliberate attempts to position its product in the customer matrix and the eventual outcome are therefore complex and dynamic.

Constructing the customer matrix

The process of constructing a customer matrix is an extremely valuable contribution to strategic thinking. I have worked with many top teams, who, relying initially on *their* perceptions of customers and their needs, have constructed customer matrices for critical segments of demand. As an initial move in the exercise it is acceptable to use management's perceptions. The thinking and debating process that is required to reach agreement invariably raises important questions about the firm's products. Consistently, the exercise of constructing the matrix demonstrates forcibly to the management team that they lack reliable and comprehensive information about their target customers and their competitors. This usually stimulates a quest for better market research.

I suggest that a management team should move through the following steps:

◆ *Clarify the target market* Be very specific in defining the target market. Sometimes it is appropriate to identify a specific customer or type of customer and a specific requirement. This avoids the tendency to generalize, which can lead to rather bland and uninteresting analyses. In selecting a specific customer it is helpful to choose one that might represent a larger group of similar people.

◆ *Identify dimensions of perceived use value* Top-team members must try to put themselves in the customer's shoes. If the team is working together, team members should initially work as individuals. Members identify what they see to be the important dimensions of perceived use value on their own, and then they share their lists. This can often reveal a wide spread of views. This indicates either that there is little real understanding of customer's needs, or that each manager may be reflecting different subsegments of demand. Once the dimensions have been pooled, the team should agree on the most critical dimensions: that is, what is most important to this customer.

◆ *Rank the dimensions of perceived use value* The selected dimensions (usually about five or six are sufficient) must then be ranked in order of importance to the customer, and weighted by allocating percentages (see Figure 2.2).

◆ *Rate competing products on each value dimension* Each product perceived by the customer to be a viable offering can be rated on a 1 to 5 scale, including the firm's product (as in Figure 2.2).

◆ *Calculate the overall perceived use value score for each product* This requires some simple arithmetic. For each product, its rating on each dimension of PUV must be multiplied by the weighting for that dimension. These are then summed to produce an overall PUV score for each product.

◆ *Plot the products on to the matrix* By combining the PUV score with the price of each product, the products can be located on to the matrix. Some adjustments of the axes may be necessary to ensure that there is an "average" position around which the products will be arrayed.

The relative simplicity of the matrix means that it is easy for managers to construct and interpret. Managers use it to discuss where they should move, where competitors are likely to move, and what would be required of the firm to shift their products in the matrix. This visual representation of the firm's competitive position in a particular market segment acts as a powerful metaphor and a focus for debate.

In Figure 2.4, I have included some examples of dimensions of perceived use value charts. The first illustrates the advantageous competitive position achieved by an oil company (T), against the best of the

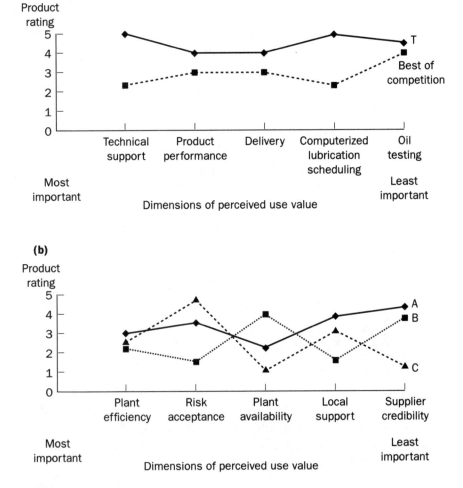

Figure 2.4 *Examples of PUV profiles: (a) supplying lubricants to paper and pulp manufacturers; (b) supplying co-generation plant to industry*

competition. This success came about through the recognition that, although the lubricants needed by the paper and pulp industry were the same as those used in the truck and bus industry, the needs of the customers were quite different. By focusing on this narrower segment, "T" have developed specific expertise that is valued by paper and pulp mill operators.

The second profile refers to customers of co-generation (heat and power) plants. The most important dimension of PUV is "plant efficiency", but the profile reveals that all competitors are judged to offer equivalent levels of efficiency. This then becomes an order-qualifying feature that is required just to be in the game. Therefore, when customers are making a choice they would focus their attention on other dimensions of PUV like financial risk acceptance, plant availability (uptime), local support and supplier credibility.

In Figure 2.5 we have a complete matrix for the supply of consumables to compact disc manufacturers. This rapidly growing market illustrates a polarization between the international players (N, M, R and D) and many "local" suppliers who are very price competitive. The problem for the firm that constructed the matrix was that they had several subsidiary companies, obtained through acquisition, that were

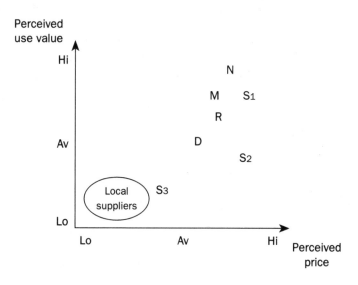

Figure 2.5 *Suppliers of consumables to CD manufacturers*

located in different parts of the matrix (the Ss). Moreover, none of the subsidiaries was in a strong position.

So what?

Before concluding the chapter with a brief summary of the arguments advanced, the following practical implications of the approach are worth noting:

- ◆ You sell to individuals, not markets, and it is dangerous to assume that all your potential customers see the world in the same way that you do.

- ◆ You need to understand what customers value, and how they assess these dimensions of value. In my experience, good-quality information about customers is not readily available in the organization, so you must obtain better information.

- ◆ Questionnaires rarely provide the depth and subtlety required. Focus groups are good, as are regular but informal discussions with customers.

- ◆ There is a strong tendency to construct convenient customer stereotypes (e.g. "all MBA students are white, male, and English, with engineering degrees and five years' management experience"). This makes life easy for us, but it is potentially dangerous. Also, there can be a strong tendency to assume we "know" what customers value, because of our long experience in the industry.

- ◆ Constructing the customer matrix does three things: first, it brings out our assumptions about customers, and what we think they value; secondly, it usually prompts a search for better information on customers and competitors; thirdly, it acts as a focal point for debate. Put simply, the matrix gives us something tangible to point at in a discussion. This may sound trivial, but it is important – as too often, strategy debates lack structure and focus.

- ◆ Analyzing customer segments to this degree can be difficult and time-consuming, so pick off the more critical segments first.

Summary

There are two basic options facing a firm seeking competitive advantage: either compete on price, or add perceived use value, although both moves can be adopted simultaneously. If the firm opts to compete on price it is vital that the firm has lower costs than its competitors. Otherwise, it is likely that, if a price war develops, price levels will reach the point where the firm is forced out of business.

In order to add perceived use value it is essential to be clear who the target customers are, and what their needs are. From this understanding the firm can develop approaches to adding perceived use values in ways that are difficult for competitors to imitate.

Whether the firm is seeking to compete on price, or to compete by adding perceived use value, it should strive to be the lowest-cost producer. The firm needs to be low cost compared with those firms the target customers perceive it to be in competition with. Achieving a low-cost position through a strategy of adding perceived use value is attainable if market share advantages enable the firm to realize the cost advantages accruing from sale and experience effects. Moreover, if the firm really understands what the customers value, then all costs that do not contribute to perceived use value can be eliminated.

A move north-east, adding perceived use value, and charging higher prices, may involve a shift from one segment to another. Care must be taken to ensure that the firm can achieve a competitive advantage over firms serving this segment.

CHAPTER 3
Sustaining advantage

Recent developments in the resource-based theory of the firm underpin the arguments developed in this chapter. (For a more thorough treatment of this approach, see the suggestions for further reading at the end of the book.) Using a resource-based perspective, the problem posed for the strategist is how to achieve a superior and sustainable position on the customer matrix described in Chapter 2, through the appropriate use and development of the firm's *competences* or capabilities.

It is unhelpful to try to identify competences without some reference to a particular product market. ''Core competences'' are only of interest if they enable a firm to compete more effectively in a given marketplace. But we shall see that it is dangerous to assume that the firm has some *generic* capabilities that can give advantage across many markets. The particular context of the firm, and the detailed way in which it conducts itself (its routines) are critical in delivering advantage.

Effecting movements in the customer matrix

As explained in Chapter 2, movements in the customer matrix are determined by changes in customer perceptions of price and perceived use value. Shifts of particular products in the matrix can occur even when the producing firm does nothing. If a competitor is able to move its product north (by adding PUV), then this has the effect of pushing other competitors' products *south* in the eyes of the customer. Products can be repositioned through changes in customer tastes and preferences that can alter the dimensions of PUV seen to be important by the customer. This may result in products well endowed with the preferred dimensions of PUV moving further north.

In addition to these spontaneous shifts in the customer matrix, firms can obviously seek to reposition their products in the matrix through deliberate acts. However, markets are in a continual state of flux, and the outcomes of actions by one producer will be moderated by actions and reactions of competitors. Competitors will not stand still, they will be attempting to effect manoeuvres in the customer matrix themselves.

Competitive imitation

As firms strive to increase or hold their sales in a given market a process of competitive imitation ensues. As one firm offers new perceived use values or higher levels of existing value dimensions they attract more customers. This forces competing firms to match these higher levels of perceived use value. Features that were once unique to one competitor become order-qualifying dimensions offered by all firms. Illustration 2.3 in the last chapter explained how Safeway had achieved advantage with its target customers by introducing keenly priced "subbrands", setting up separate parking arrangements and crèches for shoppers with young children, and introducing hand-held personal scanners to speed up the checkout process. The question facing Safeway would then be, how easy is it for competitors to copy these changes?

The competences required to compete in a given market are delivered through a complex set of activities undertaken by the firm. Some of these activities are crucial to the firm's ability to deliver value to customers. Other activities may be necessary, but they would be common to all competitors in the market. The aim for a firm must be to create a bundle of activities capable of producing a unique product that is difficult to imitate.

Grant in *Contemporary Strategy Analysis* (Blackwell, 1995) suggests that to sustain competitive advantage, strategic resources and competences need to score well when screened for four characteristics: appropriability; durability; transferability; and replicability.

Appropriability

This is concerned with the degree to which the profits earned by a particular strategic asset can be appropriated by someone other than the firm in which the profits were earned. The lower the appropriability of the asset, the more it may be able to sustain profits for the firm. An asset is difficult to appropriate if it is deeply embedded in the firm. Problems arise because firms own fixed assets, but not the skills of individuals. Thus, if in a soccer team a star develops with high goal-scoring ability, he owns that skill and is empowered either to take it to a competitor, or to use it to gain, in salary or other benefits, a high percentage of the profits from the owners of the team he represents.

However, if the profits can confidently be ascribed to the routines and team excellence developed by a wide range of managers and staff within the company, then the profits cannot be so appropriated, as the loss of any individual will not be perceived as affecting profits to any large extent. When a firm has been performing excellently over a period of time the competence may even transcend individuals or teams, and become a competence of the firm itself in an ''organizational learning'' way. Low appropriability of the strategic asset therefore means high profit sustainability.

Durability

This characteristic of a strategic asset applies not so much to its physical durability, but rather to its durability as a source of profit. The more intangible aspects of durability are therefore more important here. Shortening product and technology life cycles make most assets *less* durable than they were even a decade earlier.

However, if tangible assets are proving of declining durability as sources of sustainable profits, the more intangible distinguishing characteristics of firms are not suffering in this regard. Firms' routines and team methods can and do survive passing generations of products. Firms' reputations do not decay with the years, so long as they do not visibly decline in their essential perceived innovative, productive and high-quality characteristics. Similarly, leading brand names prove remarkably durable. As products come and go, such household names as Kelloggs, Nestlé, Du Pont, and Xerox continue with undimmed reputations in the public's eyes. Any one of these, however, can all too easily prove to have a reputation of perishable durability, given no more than a year of poor performance. The recent diminishing reputation of IBM is a salutary illustration of this.

Transferability

The easier it is to transfer the core competences and resources, the lower the sustainability of their competitive advantage. Some resources are obviously easy to transfer: for example, raw materials, employees with standard skills, machines and to some extent factories, where the transferability may be through change of ownership rather than physical transportation. In this sense, such assets are of less strategic significance, due to the ease with which they can be bought and sold. Once more the essential characteristic of a strategic asset is the degree to which it is firm-specific, embedded within the fabric of the firm, within its culture and its mode of operation. Such capabilities represent the profit-sustaining assets of the firm. The less transferable these assets, the greater their strategic profit-sustaining quality. Illustration 3.1 explains how the culture of Hewlett Packard is a source of advantage that cannot be transferred.

3.1 Imitation: the importance of socially complex resources

Illustration

Some physical resources (e.g. computers, robots, and other machines) controlled by firms are very complex. However, firms seeking to imitate these physical resources need only purchase them, take them apart, and duplicate the technology in question. With just a couple of exceptions (including the pharmaceutical and speciality chemicals industries), patents provide little protection from the imitation of a firm's physical resources. On the other hand, socially complex resources and capabilities – organizational phenomena like reputation, trust, friendship, teamwork and culture – while not patentable, are much more difficult to imitate. Imagine the difficulty of imitating Hewlett Packard's (HP) powerful and enabling culture. One of the most important components of HP's culture is that it supports and encourages teamwork and cooperation, even across divisional boundaries. HP has used this socially complex capability to enhance the compatibility of its numerous products, including printers, plotters, personal computers, mini-computers, and electronic instruments. By cooperating across these product categories, HP has been able to almost double its market value, all without introducing any radical new products or technologies.

(Source: J. B. Barney), "Looking inside for competitive advantage", *Academy of Management Executive*, vol. 9, 4 (1995), p. 55.)

Replicability

If the competence or resource cannot easily be transferred, it may be possible by appropriate investment or simply by purchasing similar assets, for a competitor to construct a nearly identical set of competences. If this is possible, the original firm possessed no real durable competitive advantage. So a profitable company will find its profits competed away, as new entrants replicate its resources and competences, and produce similar products, thereby reducing price through competition and moving the product inexorably towards commodity low-profit status. The easier the replicability, the lower the strategic importance of the resources and competences in question. Illustration 3.2 shows how Grand Metropolitan have tried to protect their brands. Part A illustrates how potentially fragile a brand may be as a source of advantage. Part B explains how far GrandMet are prepared to go to hold on to the Smirnoff brand name.

So, competences that qualify as strategic assets with profit-sustaining capacity, need to have high durability, low appropriability, transferability and replicability. Hence Grant, and others in the resource-based field, would argue that advantage can be sustained providing that the firm not only has competences which deliver valued products, but also if resources involved in delivering these competences are difficult for other firms to imitate.

However, no firm can sustain competitive advantage with the same set of resources for ever. All advantages are transitory, and ultimately all resources can either be imitated or by-passed: that is, they cease to be uniquely required to deliver value. The issue then shifts away from the prevention of imitation towards the *continual development of new sources of advantage*, a continuous process that firms neglect at their peril. Perhaps the only really sustainable advantage, as has been suggested by some commentators, is the ability to learn faster than one's rivals.

We now turn our attention to the problem of continual regeneration of sources of advantage.

Resources, systems and know-how

Discrete activities that are undertaken inside the firm combine to deliver competences. Activities themselves are combinations of three factors:

3.2 GrandMet blows its top over Asda drink lookalikes

Grand Metropolitan is taking legal action against Asda, accusing it of copying four of its best selling liqueurs and spirits. The drinks group issued a writ at the end of last week for trademark infringement.

Asda's lookalikes cost about three-quarters of the price of the originals, and GrandMet is keen to defend its brands in the vital pre-Christmas period.

"We take the integrity of our brands very seriously and see this as a serious breach of the trademark. They are clearly trying to pass off their brands as ours," said a spokesman.

Asda's Windward Coconut liqueur bears a striking resemblance to GrandMet's Malibu, down to almost identical white bottles and black screw tops. The store's Deep South comes in a similar rippled bottle to GrandMet's Southern Comfort and Asda's Daniel Boone's bourbon appears in a similar shaped bottle to GrandMet's Jack Daniel's. The fourth brand complained of is an Asda version of Archers Peach Schnapps.

Asda denies that its drinks are copycats. It claims the names and labels are different from the originals.

This is not the first time Asda has run into controversy with its products. United Biscuits served a writ against the group in October for the launch of Asda's chocolate-coated Puffin biscuits, saying customers would mistake them for its Penguin brand.

GrandMet intends to follow United Biscuits' lead and push the case through the courts on a fast-track schedule. GrandMet spends £1.2bn a year on marketing to raise the profile and differentiate its brands from own-label goods. If the courts rule in Asda's favour it would open the floodgates for other retailers.

(Source: *Observer*, 8 December 1996.)

GrandMet fails in battle royal for brand name

Grand Metropolitan has lost control of one of its premier brands after a court victory by descendants of the Russian Smirnoff family.

After years of legal battle, a Moscow arbitration court is reported to have ruled that the trademark belongs to former KGB officer Boris Smirnoff, great-grandson of Peter Smirnoff, supplier of vodka to the last tsar.

Russia's customs committee is expected to issue an order shortly that would formally ban the import of non-Russian Smirnoff vodka, accordingly to *Kommersant Daily* newspaper, which said the court made its ruling in recent days but has yet to make it public.

It remains to be seen whether GrandMet can challenge the ruling in another court. The loss of the Smirnoff brand in Russia would be a heavy blow to GrandMet because it had expected to boost sales significantly as customers move away from cheap non-branded vodka.

One executive involved in the legal fight said last night: "GrandMet has always been quite naive about the threat from Boris. They have always said they would prevail. But Boris has a lot of powerful political allies, particularly in the Moscow city government.

"The loss of the brand would be devastating. Russia is the largest vodka market in the world. GrandMet will be seen to have failed to protect one of its most valuable properties."

GrandMet sells around 15 million cases of Smirnoff every year and has exclusive right to use the name in 138 countries.

The legal skirmish has already spread to America where Boris Smirnoff and other family members have filed suit in a Delaware court asking it to declare void GrandMet's US trademarks.

GrandMet originally tried to buy off the threat from Boris Smirnoff by offering him £1m. in shares. But he refused, and started producing 100,000 bottles of vodka bearing the Smirnoff name and claiming to be the genuine article.

Boris Smirnoff has said that what is at stake is Russian pride: "Peter Smirnoff was Russian. Smirnoff belongs to us."

(Source: *Finance Guardian*, Monday, 9 June 1997.)

resources, systems and know-how, each of which typically has different characteristics.

1. *Resources* are the basic factors of production involved in the creation of a product or service. Thus materials, machinery, technology, location, premises, labour, brands and reputation may all be regarded as factors of production that are necessary before a product or service can be manufactured or performed.

2. *Systems* are the methods by which the resources are brought to life: that is, coordinated and deployed in the value activity. Systems are usually explicit and well understood, and they can often be codified into written procedures.

3. *Know-how* is the term used to represent the individual or group capability to work the systems. It is present in individuals and can be embedded throughout the

organization, but it is not codified knowledge. Know-how refers to the often implicit way things get done in the firm. Know-how includes "tacit knowledge", knowledge that enables individuals or groups to perform tasks in often superior ways, but they themselves would find it difficult to explain quite how they do what they do. For example, at the individual level, a skilled footballer or actor may not be able to explain how they perform as they do. Similarly, you may be able to ride a bike, but you would struggle to explain how to do this to someone who had never tried to ride one.

Thus resources generally are tangible and visible, with a few exceptions like reputation. At their simplest, they are land, labour and capital, the traditional factors of production of classical economics. They are, however, generally inert, and in order to be activated, they need the systems to put them to work. To be called a system, a process has to be able to be codified and summarized in a set of rules, manuals, standards, or policies.

Resources are generally imitable, but in rare cases may not be: for example, a diamond mine, or a very strong brand name. However, Illustration 3.2 showed how dependent a company can be on a brand name, particularly when it is probably the only way of differentiating a commodity product.

Systems, by definition, tend to be imitable since they are rule dominated, and can be explained and described in manuals. However, if the system is understood but not made explicit in the form of procedures or manuals – that is, it is in the form of know-how – then for a time at least it is protected against imitation.

The lowest level of imitability is generally to be found in the "know-how" category. At an extreme, only Stradivarius proved capable of making violins to such a standard that they would still be sought after by concert virtuosi hundreds of years after their manufacture. Try as he might to pass on his know-how to his apprentices, so much of the knowledge was "tacit" that he succeeded in teaching them to make only excellent violins, not superb ones.

Illustration 3.3 has extracts from an interview with Michael Grade, the former CEO of Channel 4 TV. He refers to his skills in "recognizing talent and letting them get on with it". This provides a good example of "know-how", something that possibly even Michael Grade himself

3.3 **On managing**

You have developed a considerable reputation as a scheduler. How do you make so many good judgements?
Well, scheduling is really only window-dressing. And if you take that department-store analogy a bit further, the key person is the buyer, who decides what to order for what season. Somebody then has to put it in the window in an attractive way that catches people's eyes as they pass the store, but the key person is the person who makes the judgements about what to buy to put in the window in the first place. A scheduler can't make a silk purse out of a sow's ear – the key skill is picking the right programmes and making sure they're executed well enough.

How do you do that?
Pick very good people and leave them alone, that's always been my watchword really. My skill, if I have any skill, is in recognizing talent and letting them get on with it.

Is that a general formula for success, to actually pick the right people?
Yes, absolutely. If you are a control freak and you make all the decisions yourself, how do you know if the people who are working for you are any good or not? If you're second-guessing them all the time, if anything goes wrong you can't fire anybody, you can only fire yourself. So I work absolutely on the basis of giving people as much responsibility as possible, even more responsibility than they actually want to take.

   Just to take a situation, when I arrived at Channel 4, and someone came to me with a problem, the words most often used were: "What do you think? What's your recommendation?" Then you get them used to thinking it out for themselves. Certainly you want to encourage people to come in and say "I'm not sure which way to go on this", that's a different matter, but nine times out of ten people will push the decision on to you if you let them, and you must never let them – they've got to learn to flourish on their own and stand on their own two feet.

(Source: *The Guardian*, Monday, 26 May 1997.)

This is an edited extract from *Reflections on Success*, by Martyn Lewis, published by Lennard Publishing.

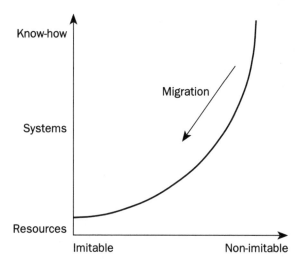

Figure 3.1 *Know-how, resources and imitability*

would not be able to explain easily to someone else, but which is clearly a source of advantage to the business. However, if this know-how resides with Mr Grade, it can of course move with him to a rival TV channel!

In general as time passes there is a tendency for know-how to migrate into systems and then often to basic resources (see Figure 3.1). Thus the know-how of the expert is observed and turned into a system by an acute analyst and system designer, and, with the passage of further time, this system may become a basic resource encapsulated in a software package, no longer unique and inimitable.

Therefore, this would suggest that firms need continually to invest in developing valued know-how. To manage this, firms need, first, to understand what customers perceive as value. Secondly, they must recognize those activities that deliver value dimensions, particularly the qualities in the product or the service that excite customers.

In Figure 3.2 we bring together the concepts discussed so far in this chapter. To recap, *competences* are a market-driven set of capabilities required by any firm to deliver perceived use value to a market segment. Competences are delivered through ongoing *activities*. These activities are combinations of *resources, systems* and *know-how*. Note that some activities that are undertaken in the firm may not contribute to

Resources Systems Know-how

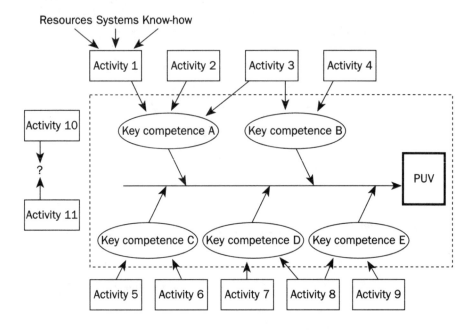

Figure 3.2 *A means–end chain*

perceived use value (activities 10 and 11 in Figure 3.2). These activities incur costs which cannot be passed on to customers, therefore they *destroy* value. Also note that some activities contribute to the delivery of more than one key competence (activities 3 and 8).

Figure 3.2 is therefore a "means–end" chain, and in constructing such a chain the management team should be able to identify value-delivering activities, and they should be able to better understand which activities are difficult for other firms to imitate. These activities will be those that not only deliver the required competences, but which also embody special know-how or resources that are unique to the firm. This means–end chain can also be used to identify activities that could easily be subcontracted, which may help in reducing costs, and will enable the firm to concentrate attention on the critical value-creating parts of the operation.

I have found that constructing a means–end chain can be useful in helping a team to understand what are the real sources of advantage that they possess. By using this straightforward structure valuable insights can be gained. Typically, groups readily identify the obvious resources and systems that combine to deliver PUV. Once these are set out on the diagram, however, useful debates are encouraged by asking questions like the following:

◆ Which activities are critical in delivering value to customers?

◆ Do we do this activity in a different way from competitors?

◆ Is it easy to imitate?

◆ Could it be done better, more cheaply, or by someone else?

Once the basic systems and resources are mapped out, attention shifts to the more intangible "know-how" sources of advantage. When group members start to say, for instance, "Oh, yes! That's right. I hadn't thought of that!", the group is beginning to draw out some of the implicit, almost subconscious things that are done to gain the firm advantage. In other words, tacit knowledge begins to become explicit knowledge.

For example, senior managers from the "pub" division of a large brewing corporation identified design skills, licence house manager (LHM) recruitment, staff motivation and cost control as being critical to success. The managers judged that they had particular success in recruiting pub managers, which prompted a vigorous discussion about why they thought they were successful in this respect. This discussion revealed that, to a large degree, identifying good potential pub managers was something of a mysterious "black art". Managers relied on intuition, instinct, or "gut feel". In an attempt to demystify this selection process, a group of regional and divisional managers were asked to select their three most successful pub managers, and to sketch out a profile of them (background, age, education, etc.), which produced some surprising results. Although some of the successful managers conformed to a stereotypical male pub manager profile, a significant number of very successful managers were: female, divorced with children, and had previous experience with major retailers (like Marks & Spencer, or Boots). These women had often ended up running the pubs after their husbands had left them, so they were in these positions through chance events. Interestingly, most of the traditional and accepted ways of recruiting managers would have bypassed these women. Although they had not been deliberately recruited, area managers had encouraged the women to take on the manager role, probably based on an implicit understanding that such people had the talent and ability to be successful.

This intuitive approach to recruiting managers would be classified as "know-how". By prompting some systematic reflection and analysis, some of this know-how can be captured, passed on to others, and may be incorporated into recruitment procedures. The questioning of these experienced managers also raised the possibility that new knowledge could be developed about recruiting different types of manager, which could be a source of advantage.

Figure 3.3 contains part of a means–end analysis undertaken by the executives of a pensions provider. The team focused on the question, "What causes success?", the aim being to better understand what it was about the firm that enabled it to be the leading pensions provider in serving the "not-for-profit" sector. Some of the causes of success are straightforward and unsurprising (e.g. factors 18, 28, and 20). However, by delving deeper into the team's understanding of the organization, some fascinating issues began to emerge. One was the critical importance of the CEO, and the firm's dependence on the particular personality, reputation and wide network of contacts that this individual brought to the role. He drove himself hard, and that set an example to all staff.

Factor 34 ("Bachelor status . . .") revealed a young, single-person subculture that, combined with the more explicit and recognizable service commitment targets, led to staff coming in voluntarily, and unpaid, at weekends to clear backlogs. This helped the team in a later debate about relocating outside of London.

Factor 33 ("Duality . . .") merited further exploration. This factor refers to the rather difficult "hybrid" status of the organization. On the one hand, they were established to serve the charitable sector, while on the other hand, their mutual trust status required them to deliver the best pensions for their members, the pension holders (i.e. the highest returns at the lowest cost). The organization therefore had not only to conduct itself in a manner acceptable to the trustees, whose values reflected their commitments to charitable and not-for-profit bodies, but it had also to be professionally managed in order to deliver the best possible returns to the pension holders. Discussing these potentially conflicting pressures uncovered previously tacit understandings about staff recruitment, management styles, and even the selection of fund managers.

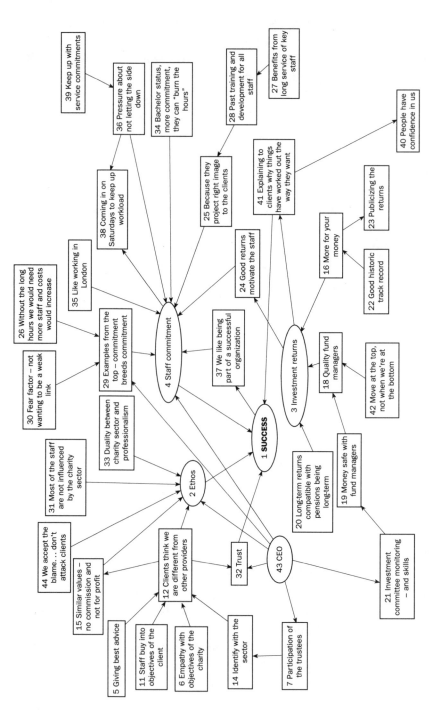

Figure 3.3 *Causes of success: a means–end analysis undertaken by a pensions provider*

Before we leave this exploration of the sources of advantage, this type of means–end analysis, though simple in essence, can point up some vital, previously tacit aspects of the organization that could easily be disturbed or destroyed by some inappropriate actions. One of the greatest dangers here is the wielding of a blunt axe in an effort to cut costs. This leads us into an exploration of cost management.

Reducing costs

Reductions in relative costs can be achieved in five ways, exploiting economies of scale; economies of scope; experience advantages; managerial efficiencies; and low factor costs. We shall consider each in turn.

Economies of scale

Economies of scale are the reductions in unit cost that are achieved by a firm increasing the scale of its activities. These economies accrue where the firm is able to spread fixed or overhead costs over a greater volume of sales, and where the scale of the firm's activities permits it to enjoy other cost advantages: for example, it is better able to bargain with suppliers to gain lower prices for its inputs. There is some empirical evidence to suggest that these scale advantages may not be widespread, and, in any event, one would not expect these economies to be universal: the extent of the advantages accruing to larger-scale production, for instance, will vary according to the technology used in the industry.

There is a view that new methods of production (e.g. flexible manufacturing systems, and "just in time" systems) may be much more important in determining relative costs than the scale of production. Firms that are able to exploit these new methods may achieve lower unit costs at relatively smaller scale than rivals (see *managerial efficiencies* below). A related concept is *economies of sequence*. Here, cost advantages accrue from linking sequential processes: an obvious example of this would be locating a hot rolling mill next to the steel blast furnace to avoid the costs of reheating the steel.

Economies of scope

Economies of scope derive from core competences. If a firm has been able to build up a competence (e.g. brand development skills) and if it is able to deploy this competence across several product markets, then it enjoys economies of scope. So scope economies are realized where a firm's competences match those required in a *number* of product markets.

Advantages from experience

Pioneering work by the Boston Consulting Group demonstrated a strong link between experience and unit cost reduction. Over time, firms accumulate experience in making or supplying products and services. If the firm learns from this experience it should be able to deliver products at lower costs by, for example, finding the most efficient ways to assemble components using method study and value engineering. Firms that have a high relative market share accumulate experience at a faster rate than their competitors. If they translate this advantage into lower unit costs, then, assuming they charge similar prices to their competitors, they should be more profitable.

Managerial efficiencies

Firms that are not subject to strong competitive pressures may suffer from "X-inefficiency". This economist's term refers to the increases in costs that can occur if firms are protected from the full rigours of a competitive market. X-inefficiency can result where firms are in a near monopoly supply position, where there is a cartel, or where a firm is protected from competition by, for example, import restrictions. Absence of competition causes a slackness in the way the firm is managed, leading to increases in input costs: for example, the amount of labour employed, excess capacity, administrative slack, and the persistence of inefficient production processes.

Some economists would argue that X-inefficiencies will exist unless there are pressures from the marketplace that force the firm's management to take action. This "survival of the fittest" argument assumes that the firm can only react to external pressures, and in the absence of these pressures, unit costs will inexorably rise.

However, a more managerialist view would suggest that firms are capable of achieving efficiency through the exercise of good management practice. Over the past decade a wide variety of management prescriptions have been proffered which could help a firm lower its costs, and which are not directly connected to scale or experience effects: for instance, total quality management practices, business process redesign, delayering, downsizing, just in time, materials requirements planning, kanban, and so on. These cost advantages can accrue where the management of a firm actively and continuously seek to drive costs out of the productive process. Even when a firm may face benign market conditions, the exercise of managerial efficiency will yield even higher levels of profit. Note that other sources of cost efficiency from scale, scope and experience effects still require the active intervention of knowledgeable management if they are to be realized. None of these volume- and scope-related advantages accrue automatically, but managerial efficiencies offer cost advantages over and above the volume-related effects.

Factor costs

Some firms will enjoy cost advantages over their rivals because they have access to cheaper resources. Many of these advantages are locational: lower wage costs; proximity to bulky raw materials; cheap power sources; low social costs (taxes etc.); having a low-valued currency. Some of these factor cost advantages can be considered as managerial efficiencies: for example, where a firm has deliberately located an assembly plant in a low wage country. Others accrue, however, through no proactive behaviour on behalf of the firm's management. Nonetheless, factor cost advantages can be so significant that they can outweigh all the hard won benefits exploited from scale, scope and experience effects.

In order to improve the relative cost position of the firm, all of these five sources of cost advantage need to be systematically explored. This means setting up teams to examine the activities set out in the means–end chain, and to look for opportunities to reduce costs, as follows:

◆ *Exploit economies of scale* By, for example, combining activities that appear in several means–end chains (e.g. after-sales servicing, training, procurement). Standardizing components can help deliver the cost advantages of larger-scale production.

◆ *Learning from experience* By using techniques like method study, value engineering, and business process re-engineering, more efficient work processes can be developed, and by codifying and proceduralizing "best practice", cost advantages can accrue.

◆ *Economies of scope* Can we leverage activities across several products or markets, like brand development, the sales force, or our corporate reputation?

◆ *Managerial efficiencies* This category covers a wide range of techniques and prescriptions that are worth investigating, like just-in-time systems, quality circles, management by objectives, materials requirements planning, TQM, and so forth.

◆ *Factor costs* Should we relocate some activities? For example, Swissair operates its reservations system from Puerto Rico, and some aerospace manufacturers have established design and development offices in India. Is it cheaper to subcontract this activity? Can we gain access to cheaper raw materials, or capital?

When exploring these potential sources of cost reduction we must always have at the front of our minds the customer's perceptions of value. This should help us guard against exploiting cost reductions which reduce the PUV of our products, and it should also help us in eliminating activities that play no part in delivering value. Some tough questions must be asked about *all* cost-incurring activities, including all management and supervisory costs.

Adding value at low cost

A rigorous analysis of PUV, leading through to a clearer insight into the competences required to compete in this particular market, can help managers focus on those activities that really matter. The resulting increase in effectiveness need not result in any cost increases. The "pub" division mentioned earlier provides a good example of adding perceived use value at low cost. One of the challenges facing the pub industry is the problem of segmenting the market and targeting the pub offer to defined market segments. Where this issue has not been confronted, the pub offering is likely to be a compromise that serves no segment particularly well.

I discovered one pub success story based on an astute manager's appreciation of his target market. The pub, located in Bristol in the west of England, was performing adequately, serving the local community in the evenings, with a few business people using it at lunchtimes. Despite the local area housing a large number of students, few used this pub. The young manager set out to attract students by tailoring the offer to meet their needs. He achieved this by buying a few board games, arranging quiz competitions, and by buying some music CDs that he believed students would like. These investments cost about £120, and over a period of months he was able to more than double the turnover of the pub.

This illustrates the importance of targeting a particular segment, and trying to understand what it is that these customers perceive as value. As a result of this attempt to target a specific market, the pub now has no business customers at lunchtimes. This is viewed as a success, because if they were in the pub, then the students might feel less at ease. Another interesting outcome has been the way other more experienced managers in the corporation have reacted to this success story. Some regard it as a fluke, this manager was just lucky. For others, this case represents a severe challenge to the accepted wisdom in their trade. The usual formula for reviving the fortunes of a pub is an extensive refurbishment costing somewhere between £50,000 and £200,000, but this case challenges this recipe. Indeed, if such a refurbishment was undertaken on this pub, that might well damage it severely in the eyes of its student customers.

A way of achieving a costless improvement in effectiveness results from corresponding improvements in managerial efficiencies. These efficiencies result from the exercise of good management practice like total quality management, re-engineering processes, just-in-time systems, and so on. Competences can be enhanced through the application of superior technologies, which, again, may not involve increases in unit costs.

Crude cost-cutting

Crude cost-cutting may have the effect of an immediate boost to the bottom line, but the longer-term effects, as the following examples demonstrate, can be catastrophic:

- ◆ Blanket cuts in budgets (e.g. "all departments have to shed 20% of staff").

- ◆ The slashing of "softer" budgets (i.e. those that do not have an immediate impact on current operations, like training, research and development).

- ◆ Simplistic delayering, where vital experience may be pushed out the door.

As relative effectiveness declines, this feeds through to the customer matrix as lower PUV. Low relative PUV forces the firm to compete on price, which adds further pressure for cost-cutting. The longer-term prognosis for a firm in this position is not good. Hence the risk of a strategy which just focuses on cost-cutting is that it may result in a reduced ability to deliver the required competences, a position that may well turn out to be irretrievable.

Cost-cutting is often an easy option to pursue. Although it may have painful consequences for the staff affected, it is a tactic that is fairly straightforward to implement. Moreover, successful implementation can be readily measured. However, if this type of crude cost-cutting is easy for you to implement, then it is probably just as easy for competitors to implement too. Therefore, this ease of imitation means that it cannot be a source of sustained advantage.

What is required is the confidence to pursue a strategy that builds advantage through enhanced competences. A management team can generate the required levels of belief in sustaining investments in competence development through thorough analysis and open debate, as we argued in the opening chapter. But dimensions of value that were once sources of advantage in the marketplace become the accepted minimum standards, and new ways to create value must be sought. As the Virgin Cola case illustrated in Chapter 2, in maturing product markets most competitors are able to reach acceptable standards of product performance. Then attention shifts to more intangible product attributes, like image and brand values, as ways of gaining advantage.

This can also be seen in the car market where advertising now focuses on issues of "lifestyle" and how a particular car can reflect an individual's personality. In a sense, therefore, the source of advantage is moving away from the physical product itself towards the product surround, where intangible benefits are stressed.

The implications of this shift of emphasis from the product core to the product surround are significant. It is not enough to have reliable products, and an efficient production process. Unless some differentiation is achieved in the mind of the customer, no sale is made. Sales can often be lost for seemingly trivial reasons, especially in business-to-business selling, where all the competing firms can meet the technical specifications required by the buyer. Then a choice is often made on some rather arbitrary criterion, of no great importance in itself, like the style of a presentation, or a rather off-hand response to a telephone enquiry. Thus the exploration of sources of advantage soon moves to dimensions of value that are difficult to measure, to evaluate and to manage. However, gaining insights into these less tangible areas of differentiation should be a source of sustained advantage because these skills are likely to be difficult to imitate.

All this suggests that by questioning our assumptions about what customers value, and by rigorously challenging our beliefs about the firm's capabilities, we can move beyond simplistic "rules of thumb" towards a more sophisticated appreciation of how we can compete in the future.

At first sight, however, Illustration 3.4 would seem to contradict the argument that it is necessary to clearly target particular customer needs, and to develop the competences to meet those needs. It would appear that Amgen are also challenging the industry recipe, focusing not on customers and markets, but on the science that produces innovation. Amgen's rather "shotgun" approach to research is helped, of course, by the two successful drugs they have previously developed. Maybe this reflects the peculiarities of the pharmaceutical industry: you need some luck to hit on a successful drug, but the odds on winning the lottery improve if you can buy thousands of tickets! The cost implications of "shotgun" research are staggering, of course, so identifying the right kind of research to invest in becomes *the* critical competence, not the research effort per se.

So far we have restricted our analysis to firms competing within one market segment. We made this assumption to simplify the argument.

We now consider the more typical case of firms competing in several market segments.

3.4 Smart science

Illustration

Unlike its rivals, biotech leader Amgen emphasizes lab research – not market research.

Business people are surrounded by a cacophony of voices, and one key to innovative strategy is to listen to new ones. That's what CEO Gordon Binder did at Amgen, whose 68 per cent average annual return over the past decade leads the *FORTUNE 1,000*. Drug companies succeed or fail based on a handful of blockbuster drugs. Amgen, for example, has only two drugs on the market – one helps dialysis patients; the other is an immune-system booster that helps people fight infections – but each brings in a billion dollars per year. With economics like that and with many projects crying out for investment, you have to pick which voices to hear.

Conventional wisdom says listen to the market. Says Binder: "Most pharmaceuticals companies, and quite a few biotech ones as well, are basically market-driven. They see that large numbers of people have a particular disease and decide to gather some scientists to do something about it."

Amgen heard things differently. Rather than start with the disease and work back to the science, Amgen assumed that the opposite strategy is superior – that companies should take brilliant science and find a unique use for it. The company's immune booster, for instance, helps keep the side effects of chemotherapy from killing cancer patients.

Starting with the science helps in other ways too. Each year the feds pour untold millions into universities and hospitals for medical research. "That kind of money will produce a lot of interesting things," says Binder.

To get a piece of it – and to bring in still more new voices – Amgen has collaborative arrangements with about 200 colleges and universities. It looks like one of those will pay off big. Last year at Rockefeller University, a professor discovered that a gene – now licensed by Amgen – may yield new treatments for obesity. Talk about potential blockbusters – more than 20 per cent of adults in the US are clinically obese; along with others who think they're chubby, they spend upwards of $30bn a year to shed pounds. Just a small percentage of that could plump up Amgen's bottom line even more.

(Source: *FORTUNE*, 23 June 1997.)

Competing across segments

Figure 3.4 represents the situation of a firm competing in four different market segments. The competences required to compete successfully in each segment are represented by letters A to M. So the key competences required in segments 3 and 4 are similar in that competences A, B and C appear in both competence profiles. Our firm, relative to competitors is well endowed with competences A, B and C. We could refer to these, then, as its *core competences*.

We would expect the firm to perform well in market segments 3 and 4, as its core competences match three of the key competences required.

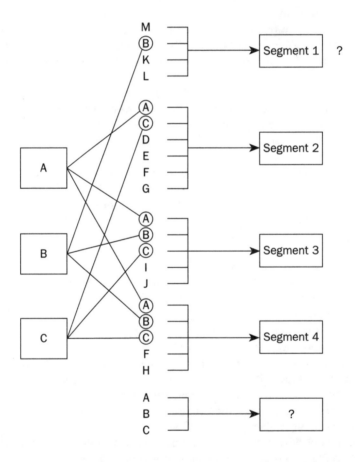

Figure 3.4 *Developing core and key competences in four market segments*

It may be less well positioned in segments 1 and 2, although it may be that none of its competitors is particulary strong in the delivery of these competences.

By leveraging its core competences across four market segments the firm may be achieving economies of scope. And, as indicated at the foot of Figure 3.4, there may be possibilities to explore other markets which require competences A, B and C. Here, therefore, it would be an approach to diversification that would be driven by an understanding of the firm's core competences.

However, there may be some dangers in overextending the scope of the firm in this way. For example, let us assume that a large grocery retailer has a core competence in negotiating with suppliers. This competence may have been developed over time through the corporation's dealings with large food manufacturers and household product suppliers. They then diversify by stocking *clothes* in their larger stores. To succeed with this diversification the firm needs to possess the appropriate competences, which includes competence in negotiating with suppliers. However, negotiations with clothing manufacturers have peculiarities that are outside the firm's experiences in dealing with grocery suppliers: for instance, most of the clothing manufacturers are located in the Far East, and the style of negotiation is subtly different. So, although the retailer has competence in negotiation, this is not a *generic* competence: it is actually specific to certain market segments. Moreover, attempts to develop a generic competence may reduce the firm's ability to perform outstandingly in any one specific segment.

This is why unravelling in fine detail the causes of current success, using means–end diagrams like Figure 3.3, is so important. There are other examples where managers have believed the firm possessed a core competence that could be transferred to a related product market, only to discover that the incumbent competitors could outperform them. This was because the incumbents not only had the competence as a generic capability, but they had also refined, developed and honed this expertise in the particular marketplace. Two examples spring to mind. The first was Lex Services' move into managing hotels, premised on the assumption that the competences required to manage retail motor sales and service outlets were the same as those required to run hotels. The logic is appealing on first inspection: they are service businesses; both types of operation are conducted in dispersed locations; and they both involve high customer contact. But people running hotels understand the business at a *detailed* level; they understand the basic *routines* of the business, and how a successful hotel *feels*.

The second example comes from the USA. When Philip Morris, manufacturers of Marlboro cigarettes, acquired Miller, the brewing corporation, they were able to transform the performance of this rather sleepy mid-ranked brewer into number two in the USA, behind Anheuser-Busch. They succeeded primarily because Philip Morris's skills in brand development, when applied to the beer market, gave Miller a competitive edge. But the trick did not work when they took over 7 Up, the soft-drinks manufacturer. Philip Morris's marketing skills were still excellent, but in the soft-drinks industry they were pitched against Coca-Cola and Pepsi, who had excellent marketing skills that had been developed and refined *in the soft-drinks industry*. So be wary of assuming that a competence can be easily transferred to a different product market. The detail matters, routines are important, and the intangible, cultural elements of the organization can make all the difference.

As well as assuming that firms compete in a single product market, we have also tended to simplify competitor actions and reactions to the firm's strategic manoeuvres. We now extend our exploration by considering likely competitor responses to the firm's actions.

Competitor actions and reactions

The customer matrix recognizes the dynamic nature of all product markets. In this section we consider competitor actions and reactions.

The first mover in an industry is usually able to achieve a strong and lasting competitive advantage over laggard firms. We can see from our consideration of cost advantages where some of the first-mover benefits derive from. The first mover is able to build a large market share early on. This allows the firm to exploit volume-related economies (of scale and experience) earlier than followers, thus permitting a more aggressive pricing strategy, which builds more share, and so on.

If a competitor is also playing an aggressive game, however, although the absolute advantages from volume effects may accrue, there may be little or no *relative* cost advantage. In other words, as the firm lowers unit costs, the average cost level in the industry is falling at the same rate. So the outcome may be lower unit costs for the firm, but no *relative* cost advantage.

Similarly, improvements in key competences may result in no relative advantages accruing. The key issue here is the ease with which competitors can improve their competence endowments.

First-mover advantages can of course lead to moves north which cannot be readily imitated. It may be the case that a particular firm has been able to improve its competences in a way which is very difficult for other firms to emulate. This could be due to the particular path pursued by the firm over time, which has enabled it to accumulate valuable know-how. Rival firms may therefore need to follow similar patterns of development over time, and there is little scope for followers to compress the time it takes to acquire this learning.

Changes in technology, resulting in a shift in the mix of key competences required to compete in a market, can take a firm by surprise. New entrants can have a similar effect, especially if they are able to acquire the most efficient and effective resources to compete. This will raise the average level of competence endowment, and lower average unit costs.

Scope advantages may also permit some firms performing in a product market to achieve effectiveness and cost positions that cannot be matched by more narrowly focused competitors.

So what?

Some practical issues that have arisen when teams have applied the approaches set out in this chapter are as follows:

♦ Managers do not normally think in terms of competences, and when they do, they often adopt a very functional approach to defining them: for example, "marketing competence", "production capacity". This can be a starting point, but usually the competences required to be effective span *across* the organization, like "new product development", or "responsiveness to customer needs". So the team should be encouraged to look beyond the functional structure of the firm when analyzing competences.

♦ Only short-term cost advantage can derive from axing budgets and reducing head count. Teams should prepare to *systematically* explore sources of cost advantage that can accrue from scale, scope, experience, managerial efficiencies and factor costs.

◆ Constructing the "means–end" chain, which identifies activities that combine to deliver perceived use value to customers, usually promotes a lively debate. Once managers have identified the more obvious activities, and the resources and systems that make up each activity, attention can shift to more challenging questions: Which of these activities really delivers added value to customers? How easy is it to imitate? Which activities could be safely subcontracted? How can these activities be done better, or cheaper?

Critical practical issues stemming from the resource-based perspective are as follows:

◆ Inadequate physical resources and poor systems will be a source of *disadvantage*, but correcting them cannot confer an enduring *advantage* because they can be easily imitated. Unfortunately, managers are much more comfortable debating these resource issues than they are in addressing the more intangible sources of advantage like "know-how".

◆ An awareness of tacit knowledge, embedded routines and "cultural" sources of advantage can sensitize management to these less tangible aspects of the firm's competences. This should raise questions about what these would be in *our* firm, and how they could be enhanced as sources of advantage. It should also alert us to the dangers of inadvertently destroying an intangible source of advantage, particularly through overzealous cost-cutting.

◆ *Detail matters.* For example, you could compare two management schools and you may discover that 95 per cent of what you see is the same: they run the same courses, have the same organization structure, lecture rooms are the same, library facilities are comparable, and so forth. Yet one is far more successful than the other. The performance gap may well derive from subtle and difficult-to-identify differences in atmosphere, morale, and shared values or leadership. At the basic routine level of day-to-day activity, the culture of the organizations is critically different. We take up these issues further in the following two chapters.

Remember that the techniques explained in this book are merely *tools for thought and debate*, they help to structure and shape our discussions. They are not precise, nor can they produce "answers". Be prepared to adapt them to suit your particular circumstances.

Summary

In this chapter we have addressed the *delivery* of perceived use value from a resource-based perspective. Advantage is gained by moving in the customer matrix. In order to affect the firm's PUV and price position the firm needs to have the appropriate core competences. Competences are made up of activities, which in turn are bundles of resources, systems and know-how.

However, to add the quality of sustainability to that of competitive advantage, the firm's competences need to be as close to inimitable as possible. Generally, this is more likely to be in the tacit know-how of individuals and teams, rather than in the readily codifiable systems or inert resources.

Towards the end of the chapter we explicitly addressed the actions and reactions of competitors. Finally, we extended the analysis to consider situations where the firm competes in a variety of product markets.

CHAPTER 4

The competitive environment

In this chapter we explore techniques that can be used to develop insights into the competitive situation in a particular market segment. A segment is defined as a group of customers who have similar needs, and share similar perceptions of use values that would meet their needs. Thus a segment of demand could span across geographic boundaries: that is, there might be people with very similar needs ranged across the globe. What unites them are perceptions that they have the same or similar needs, and that there are no barriers to prevent them being offered the same range of products.

In most strategy texts "environmental appraisal" is conducted *before* the exploration of possible competitive strategies. I have adopted a different sequence in this book for the following reasons:

◆ An unfocused, general appraisal of the environment usually provides little insight.

◆ In process terms, beginning with environmental appraisal rarely excites or energizes the team.

◆ Broadbrush trends and issues identified in the appraisal rarely feed through to affect strategic decisions. These issues are usually judged to be important, but they are conceptually remote in time and space from the immediate concerns of the managers.

It is therefore more productive to focus on the analysis of specific market segments first, using the customer matrix, before considering how these segments may evolve in the future. In this way, when the environmental analysis is carried out, the team have a much clearer focus on the kinds of questions they want answers to.

There are two critical issues at segment level:

1. *The nature of the effective demand* What is the nature of this demand in the segment? What are the needs of customers? What is the volume of demand? Is demand growing or shrinking?

2. *Competence imitability* How easy is it for firms to replicate the key competences required to meet the demand?

Prices and cost levels combine to indicate the overall mass of profit that might be generated by the aggregate of firms operating in the segment. Firm-level profitability will be critically affected by the ease with which the competences required to compete in the segment can be imitated. The easier it is for the competences to be imitated, the more firms are likely to be attracted into serving the segment. If demand is increasing in the segment, prices and profits may be rising as well. If it is relatively easy for a new firm to enter the market segment, the number of firms will increase, the likely outcome being a reduction in profitability for each individual firm.

The ease with which other firms can enter a market affects the balance of power between an individual firm and customers. More choice of suppliers gives the customer bargaining power over the firm. If the firm is in a strong position, perceived by customers as offering a unique and valued product, the firm is able to charge higher prices and/ or sell to more customers than its competitors.

In order to understand the situation within a particular market segment, it is necessary to be able to identify the "drivers of demand": that is, what factors affect the level of effective demand in the segment. We also need to understand the factors that affect competence imitability, which we shall refer to as the "drivers of imitability".

Drivers of demand

We need to know what determines the level of demand within a particular segment. This question can be broken down into two further questions:

1. What influences customer needs in the segment?

2. What influences the number of customers in the segment?

In trying to assess the influences on customer needs we require to know a good deal about the customer. A straightforward distinction can be made between customers purchasing on behalf of businesses (i.e. business customers) and customers purchasing for their own or their family's consumption. Typically, business customers are purchasing goods and services as inputs to a business process (e.g. components, power, computer software, short-term finance, liability insurance). In order to better understand the drivers of demand for business customers we have to gain insights into *their* businesses, particularly their needs and how our products and services can meet those needs. We must be able to anticipate how these needs may change in the future, and also whether the number of potential business customers will increase or decrease. This requires a sophisticated knowledge of the customer's industry, *their* competitors, and *their* customers. In fact, you have to know nearly as much about your business customer's business as you should know about your own.

Some firms have been particularly diligent in this regard. Major suppliers of computer hardware have been attempting to redefine their businesses from being suppliers of hardware, to becoming providers of systems and solutions to their clients. In effecting this transformation, one corporation, AT&T, has realized that it needs to be involved in the very early phases of strategic decision-making in client organizations, which has led, in turn, to important training and development initiatives designed to transform their sales force into credible strategic-level consultants. To achieve this, their consultants have to be able both to analyze the strategic positioning of their target clients, and to contribute to strategy debates within client organizations.

In personal customer segments we have to be able to understand their needs, and how these might change in the future. I have found that these questions are extremely difficult to answer. To make progress with this analysis we have to comprehend the different layers of needs, not just the more straightforward, obvious motivations that drive customers. We must then identify what trends – social, demographic and economic – affect these needs. This might suggest how the needs may change in the future, and whether the demand within the particular segment is likely to increase or decrease.

Drivers of imitability

I have labelled the factors that influence the ease with which firms can imitate the key competences required to compete in a segment the "drivers of imitability". Clearly, these factors will differ from one segment to another, but based on our discussion in Chapter 3 they will stem from the following sources:

◆ The transparency of the process: that is, how easy it is for an outsider to understand the business processes required to operate in the segment.

◆ Access to critical resources and systems including resource inputs, brands, reputation, installed base, and access to channels of distribution.

◆ Economies of scale, scope and experience.

◆ Technical know-how.

These factors have been variously referred to as barriers to imitation, mobility barriers, or barriers to entry. As we argued earlier, the ease with which new firms are able to enter a market is a critical determinant of the overall attractiveness of a segment. We therefore need to understand, for a particular segment, what affects these barriers to imitability.

There are some existing frameworks and techniques that can help us shed some light on the two issues of demand, and of competence imitability, as follows:

1. The structural analysis of industries which analyzes the forces of competition within an industry (Michael Porter's "Five Force" analysis).

2. Competitor analysis: that is, a detailed assessment of individual competitors.

3. PEST analysis, for analyzing the macroenvironment.

The first two techniques should help us to address primarily the issue of competence imitability. PEST analysis can help us to explore how segment demand may change in the future. We briefly explain these approaches in this chapter, and at the end of the chapter we examine the extent to which the techniques have been able to illuminate the two critical issues of demand and imitability.

Structural analysis of industries

In his book, *Competitive Strategy* (Free Press, 1980), Michael Porter develops what has become a very popular framework for analyzing the structure of an industry or market segment, from the viewpoint of its attractiveness to a player already in the industry. For the purposes of this analysis, an industry is defined as a group of firms producing similar goods or services for the same market. Porter's approach concentrates on the competitive forces operating in the industry, the outcome of the analysis being an assessment of the attractiveness of the industry, defined by how profitable the industry is likely to be for the firms already in it. The real benefit of the approach is that it forces the management team to view the industry from a broader perspective than would typically be the case. The discipline of assessing the relative strengths of the forces operating in the industry can develop new and important insights into the competitive environment, which can help in the construction of better competitive strategies.

Porter argues that there are five competitive forces which operate in an industry and together they determine the potential profitability of that industry. The five forces are as follows:

1. Rivalry among existing firms.

2. The barriers to new entrants.

3. The bargaining power of buyers.

4. The bargaining power of suppliers.

5. The threat from substitute products or services.

Each will be considered in turn. Figure 4.1 sets out a schematic check list of the forces.

Rivalry

Rivalry refers to the intensity of competitive behaviour within the industry. It addresses such issues as whether firms are continually seeking to outmanoeuvre their rivals through price cuts, new product innovations, advertising, credit deals, or promotional campaigns. Or

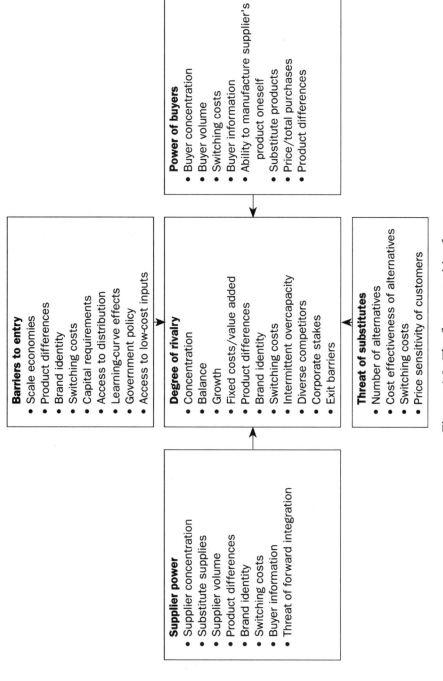

Barriers to entry
- Scale economies
- Product differences
- Brand identity
- Switching costs
- Capital requirements
- Access to distribution
- Learning-curve effects
- Government policy
- Access to low-cost inputs

Supplier power
- Supplier concentration
- Substitute supplies
- Supplier volume
- Product differences
- Brand identity
- Switching costs
- Buyer information
- Threat of forward integration

Degree of rivalry
- Concentration
- Balance
- Growth
- Fixed costs/value added
- Product differences
- Brand identity
- Switching costs
- Intermittent overcapacity
- Diverse competitors
- Corporate stakes
- Exit barriers

Power of buyers
- Buyer concentration
- Buyer volume
- Switching costs
- Buyer information
- Ability to manufacture supplier's product oneself
- Substitute products
- Price/total purchases
- Product differences

Threat of substitutes
- Number of alternatives
- Cost effectiveness of alternatives
- Switching costs
- Price sensitivity of customers

Figure 4.1 *The five competitive forces*

whether perhaps there is little competitive activity, and firms are content to stick with their shares of the market and unwilling to upset the balance of the industry by, say, instigating a price war.

There are a number of factors which, Porter suggests, determine the probable intensity of rivalry in an industry, as follows:

- ◆ *Slowing growth of demand, or declining demand* If demand slows, firms can only maintain historic growth rates by gaining market share from competitors. This tends to intensify rivalry as firms battle for market share by price cuts or other attempts to boost sales. Declining demand will lead to further intensification of competitive activity, particularly if there are *exit* barriers to the industry. These barriers can take the form of large investments of capital that has no alternative use, few transferable skills, and high costs of plant closure including redundancy costs. It is important to note that this factor refers not to slow growth itself, but to the slowing of growth in the absence of the exit of any competitors.

- ◆ *High fixed costs* If the cost structure of the industry is such that there is a high fixed cost, and a low marginal cost component, then firms will be under intense pressure to produce near full capacity. If demand falls off, therefore, firms will use price cuts and other weapons to maintain sales. Similar behaviour can occur in industries with highly perishable products.

- ◆ *Unpredictable and diverse competitors* If the industry is made up of a diverse group of firms, their behaviour is likely to be unpredictable. If there are new entrants from other countries or industries who do not play by the "rules", their maverick behaviour will probably lead to an extremely volatile competitive arena.

- ◆ *Low switching costs* Switching costs are costs incurred by the buyer in moving from one supplier to another. For example, switching costs are incurred if an airline moves from an all Boeing fleet to a mixed Airbus/Boeing fleet: for example, the need for crew training, spares inventories, and so forth. If switching costs are low in an industry, buyers are able to switch between suppliers without any penalty. Switching costs may be tangible, as in the airline example, or may be composed of the intangible costs evolving from being accustomed to working smoothly with a particular supplier.

♦ *A commodity product* The more a firm is able to differentiate its product either by establishing a strong brand name or by offering clearly distinct PUV, the less it needs to fear its rivals, as it is laying claim to the argument that it alone supplies a given market need. Correspondingly, the nearer its product is to being a commodity, the greater is likely to be the rivalry it faces. Brand names therefore tend to reduce rivalry since they emphasize differentiation, and establish at least psychological switching costs for the consumer if he or she is to move to a different brand. IBM has 100 per cent of the market for IBM computers after all, and always will have!

♦ *Cyclicality leading to periodic overcapacity* During these periods of spare capacity, rivalry will be intense as firms fight to fill their factories.

♦ *High corporate stakes* In difficult times, the options are ''fight or flight''. If the market is an important one to the main players in it they will be inclined to fight. This will also be the case if exit costs are high, or if it is critical to gain a dominant position early on in an emerging industry (e.g. VHS versus Betamax, Microsoft versus Apple's Macintosh).

Barriers to entry

If new firms enter an industry they bring additional capacity. If demand is not increasing to absorb this additional capacity, then the new entrants will have to compete for a share of the existing demand. To gain entry they may either compete with lower prices or with enhanced PUV or both. The net effect of these new entrants will probably be to lower the overall level of profitability in the industry. Entry is deterred by the presence of barriers to entry, which can stem from a number of sources. We have already considered some of these barriers in our discussion of imitability, but for completeness we set out the barriers identified by Porter, as follows:

♦ *Economies of scale* If there are major cost advantages to be gained from operating at a large scale, then new entrants will either have to match that scale, or have higher unit costs and suffer lower margins. Scale economies are usually thought of as a production phenomenon, but may also exist in advertising, purchasing, R&D, after-sales services and elsewhere.

◆ *Experience benefits* Low unit costs can be achieved by accumulated learning: that is, finding progressively more efficient ways of doing things, which, if they are significant, would place inexperienced new entrants at a unit cost disadvantage.

◆ *Access to know-how* Patents can protect firms from new entrants, and difficulties in accessing process knowledge and particular skills can be substantial barriers to entry.

◆ *Customer brand loyalty* Customers may have preferred brands, or they may have strong relationships with their existing suppliers, which they are reluctant to break. New entrants would have to persuade customers that it was worth their while incurring these switching costs involved in moving to the product of a new entrant. This may provide a strong barrier to entry.

◆ *Capital costs of entry* If capital costs are high, this will limit the number of potential entrants. Such costs include setting up production facilities, research and development costs, establishing dealer networks and initial promotion expenses.

◆ *High switching costs* If customers will incur high switching costs if they move to a new entrant's product, this constitutes a barrier to entry. Thus, if IBM have a high installed base in the mainframe computer market, this constitutes a very effective barrier to the entry of other potential rivals, as winning orders against the supplier of the installed base would require a really special advantage to overcome the switching costs of changing computer systems.

◆ *Government policy* Government policy may also provide a barrier to entry as the government seeks to regulate the industry by restricting licences, issuing exclusive franchises, or establishing regulations that are onerous and costly to implement.

◆ *Access to low-cost inputs* Entry by potential competitors will be difficult without such access. For example, low labour costs in the Far East have provided barriers to the future development of textile industries in the developed world.

Bargaining power of buyers

Customers/buyers can have considerable bargaining power for a variety of reasons. For example:

◆ When there are *few buyers,* and they purchase in large quantities.

◆ When the buyers have *low switching costs,* and therefore probably low loyalty. Highly differentiated products offer less opportunity for the exercise of buyer power than do relatively undifferentiated products.

◆ When buyers face *many relatively small sellers.*

◆ When the item being purchased is *not an important* one for the buyer, and therefore he or she can take it or leave it.

◆ When they have a lot of *information* concerning competitive offers, which they can use for bargaining.

◆ When there is a real risk that the buyer's firm may decide to *integrate backwards*: that is, to make the product itself rather than buy it in.

Thus where buyers are faced with many alternatives, and the cost of switching is low or non-existent, buyers have power. The more concentrated the buyers, the greater their power. Buyer power is normally evidenced by the ability of the buyer to bargain the price downwards.

Bargaining power of suppliers

Correspondingly, the ability of suppliers to increase prices without losing sales illustrates *their* power. Such power may come about in the following circumstances:

- ◆ When the purchase is *important* to the buyer.

- ◆ When buyers have *high switching costs.*

- ◆ When there are *few alternative sources* of supply.

- ◆ When any particular buyer is *not an important customer* of the supplier.

- ◆ When there is the real risk that the supplier may *integrate forward*: for instance, instead of the car maker supplying its independent dealers, it may decide to set up its own dealer subsidiary.

Examples of powerful supplier relationships would be gas supply to the glass container industry, and microchip suppliers to the computer industry. Illustration 4.1 explains the changing relationship between the car manufacturers and their component suppliers as the manufacturers face increasing rivalry.

The term "suppliers" includes the providers of capital and of specialist skills. Hence, if an industry is dependent on particularly skilled people, these individuals can bargain up their pay levels: for example, advertising agencies are highly dependent on a few creative individuals, and their pay is accordingly high.

If suppliers are powerful they can increase the prices of their inputs, thus extracting potential profits from the industry. If firms are facing both powerful suppliers *and* buyers, profits will be severely squeezed, as input cost increases cannot be passed on in higher prices to buyers. Such a situation is likely to make the industry unattractive to potential entrants.

Threat of substitutes

Industries are usually defined in terms of the products or services they provide. Hence, we have the aluminium can industry, the sugar industry, or the pizza restaurant industry. This enables us to identify a group of firms doing similar things who would see themselves as being in competition with each other. However, if we define industries from the *buyer's* perspective, we might come up with a quite different set of firms, who do not provide similar products, but who do nevertheless meet the same types of buyer needs. The buyer who likes sweet coffee might

4.1 Supply chain hit hard by cost squeeze

The relationship between the auto industry and its suppliers has tilted irrevocably in favour of the manufacturers in recent years, says Haig Simonian.

There are few sadder sights than an abandoned car stripped of its parts. While the desolate shell evokes mobility, the skeleton highlights the inadequacy of what remains when wheels, dashboard, seats and countless other components are torn away. Something similar describes the evolving relationship between vehicle manufacturers and their suppliers. While the former fire the imagination, they would be marooned without the latter. Outside suppliers account for between 65 per cent and 75 per cent of the value of a vehicle: without them, the car industry would be immobile.

In spite of that dependence, the relationship between the auto industry and its suppliers has tilted irrevocably in favour of the manufacturers in recent years. Recession, competition and overcapacity have forced vehicle manufacturers to squeeze their costs. With components accounting for such a large proportion of expenditure, the supply chain has been hardest hit. But cost-cutting is just one of the three crucial trends shaping the world components industry. New legislation, which has stimulated demand for additional safety and environmental features, and stiffening competition within the industry, which has sharpened the importance of research and development, are the two others. Take relations with the auto industry first. Alongside the universal priority of cost controls, many leading vehicle manufacturers have been internationalizing their output, obliging suppliers to accompany them across the globe.

Cost-reduction and internationalization has spurred rationalization on the components side. As the car companies have stressed economies of scale by handing out more business to fewer suppliers, the components industry has been restructuring into a number of multinationals concentrating on a tight range of specialities. Ford has been the catalyst. Its Ford 2000 strategy of simplifying product development has galvanized the components industry. Many observers expect the trend to be reinforced as other vehicle manufacturers try to improve their cost bases and find growth opportunities outside the mature markets of the US, Japan and Europe.

Cost pressures in the car industry have also stimulated the development of more complex components and a new, less adversarial, relationship between component makers and their customers. At the extreme, car and component companies have started collaborating from the dawn of a new vehicle project to reduce costs. Suppliers have been told about the new product and then given virtual carte blanche to come up with the goods. Such outsourcing has transferred part of the R & D overhead from vehicle makers to their suppliers and given the latter the chance to devise more radical solutions. Even when components suppliers are only called in at a later stage, they have honed their competitiveness by combining their products into complete subassemblies rather than individual parts. Such subassemblies, which could be as simple as a bunch of electric wires linked together in a harness, are easier and faster to fit on the assembly line than a maze of confusing cables.

(Source: *FT Survey, Automotive Components*, 29 June 1995.)

consider manufacturers of sugar and of artificial sweeteners to be in direct competition. A lunchtime shopper may see a pizza restaurant, a hamburger outlet, a pub and a delicatessen selling sandwiches as being in direct competition for his or her custom.

Substitute products are alternative ways of meeting buyer needs. In this respect, the fax machine provides a substitute for the letter but not for parcel post, and E-mail is a substitute threat to the fax. The effect of substitute products on the previously product-defined industry is to place a ceiling on prices, since a price rise may cause a previously loyal customer to shift to the substitute product. Furthermore, no purchase at all may have the same effect as that of a substitute product, since both represent a reduction of effective demand from the industry.

The threat of substitutes is high in the following situations:

◆ When there are a number of equally cost-effective ways of meeting the same customer need.

◆ When the customer faces few switching costs in moving to the substitute product.

◆ When the customer exhibits high price sensitivity, and the substitute has a low price.

Illustration 4.2 points out the potential threat of substitute products or services. Asking questions about substitutes focuses attention on the underlying *needs* of the customer, an issue that we stressed in Chapter 2.

Defining the boundaries of an industry is more an art than a science, but it is crucial to an accurate assessment of industry attractiveness. If an overly narrow product-based definition is adopted, there are risks that

4.2 **The threat of substitutes**

Illustration

What unrecognized issues lurk in the background of other businesses? Almost everywhere you look, there is a challenge that existing competitors are not yet ready to face. In computers, for example, no one in the industry has yet come to terms with a fundamental change in customers' needs.

They don't want to buy computers any more: instead, they want effortless, low-cost, transparent information processing, distributed throughout their companies and homes. They want all the rest of the hoo-ha – the standards battles, the product choices, the compatibility issues – to go away. Locked in a struggle for market dominance, the industry is not ready to recognize it yet. But eventually, someone will, setting a pattern for the industry in the next century.

In cars, the issue is distribution, responsible for nearly half the value added. The old system of small, franchised dealerships is cracking up. There are lots of tentative stabs at a new framework: car sales on the Internet, auto superstores, Daewoo's wholly owned distribution chain in the UK, Ford's possible introduction of direct sales in Indianapolis. But so far, they are just straws in the wind, an indication that everybody in the industry knows about the issue – but that none of the big boys is yet ready to make a wholesale commitment to a new approach.

In financial services, the issue is the potential disappearance of most of the physical manifestations of banking. When customers switch the loyalty in their banking relationship from an institution to a budget programme running on their home PCs, the industry will be transformed.

So far, most big banks are treating this with extreme caution, confining their experiments to telephone banking or proprietary electronic systems. At some point, though, one of the big players will switch to a standard program like Intuit's Quicken or Microsoft Money. At that moment, retail banking will change forever. Until it does, the industry is pretending the problem doesn't exist.

(Source: *Financial Times*, 15 May 1997.)

the analysis will miss critical aspects of the competitive environment. Some industries are geographically fragmented, with each locality having just one or two producers (e.g. quarries, cinemas, zoos, or regional newspapers). In most respects, similar firms in different regions are not direct competitors. Therefore, one of the key decisions to make in a five-force analysis is the choice of industry boundary. The market is not an arbitrary one, it is a ''strategic market'': that is, one supplying a distinct customer-determined need to a geographically defined customer group. Whether it be local, regional, national, pan-national, the characteristics of the market will determine which of these types of market is appropriate for a particular analysis. Thus, although the corrugated cardboard market is said to be limited to a fifty-mile radius of the producer for reasons of transport costs in relation to an undifferentiated product, the market for video recorders can be legitimately regarded as global. The five-force analysis boundaries adopted must reflect these different facets if the analysis is to be useful for generating insights into possible competitive strategies.

Managers can of course redefine their ''industry'' by operating on the five forces themselves (e.g. developing brand names, creating switching costs). In other words, by developing and sustaining competitive advantage, the industry structure is redefined: for example, rivalry is reduced, entry becomes more difficult, buyers have less power, and so forth.

Advantages of the five-forces framework

The main benefit of using this technique is that it provides a structure for management thinking about the competitive environment. Each force can be examined using the check lists set out above. Some aspects will be highly relevant to the industry and some less relevant. Some valuable insights into the nature of the industry will usually emerge from such analysis.

It can also be useful if two or more groups of managers carry out an appraisal independently. Differences of perceptions can then be raised and discussed, and where agreement is reached, some confidence can be placed in the judgements.

Several industry/market analyses will often be worthwhile. The first would be for the industry as a whole, while subsequent analyses would focus on particular segments. A third round might consider the industry at some defined point in the *future*, in order to introduce a dynamic element into what has so far been an exercise in analyzing the current situation. The framework can then be productive in helping to define strategic segment boundaries, in revealing insights about the key forces in the competitive environment, and in identifying which forces can be transformed into advantageous ones by operating proactively upon them: for example, by creating switching costs, or in establishing stronger barriers to entry by building strong brand names.

Further advantage is possible through rating the strength of each of the five forces. This will help to focus attention on the main competitive factors in each segment, and to compare the attractiveness of each segment. A simple points system would be: 1 = a weak force, 5 = a strong force. Under such a schema an "attractive" industry would be one scoring 12 points or less. The disadvantage of such a simplistic system is that it assumes each force is equally important. But in, for example, a patent-dominated industry, or a defence industry, barriers to entry, or supplier power respectively would merit above-average weighting. However, this could be allowed for in an amended scoring system.

Illustration 4.3 sets out the problems facing the Pearson Group. This conglomerate has businesses that compete in a wide range of product markets, from newspapers, through TV to banking. Emily Bell recommends that Pearson should focus on one type of business. In making a choice of where it should be operating, a sound understanding of the markets Pearson currently competes in would be beneficial. Then they could assess the extent to which Pearson have the competences to compete successfully in each of these markets. This would also help them identify their *core* competences, which they could leverage across different group businesses. Clearly, though, Pearson is facing *corporate* strategy problems, something we address in Chapter 8.

Five-forces analysis provides useful insights into the structure of an industry, but it is more valuable to be able to look ahead, to predict how these forces might change in the future. What the analysis gives us is a "snapshot" of the industry's structure at one point in time; what we need is the injection of a dynamic element into the model.

Industry life cycle

The stage of an industry's development can influence the nature of competitive rivalry. For instance, in the early days of a new industry there are usually many new entrants. They are joining a growing industry where demand is outstripping supply, and consequently, the firms can meet their growth aspirations without poaching customers

4.3 **Publish, and broadcasting be damned**

Emily Bell has three words of advice for the new chief executive of Pearson: focus, focus and focus.

Marjorie Scardino has enjoyed a healthy reputation and considerable success in guiding the *Economist* magazine to a successful performance on both sides of the Atlantic, but running a limited-circulation magazine and refocusing Pearson are challenges of an altogether different magnitude.

Righting Pearson means understanding precisely what is wrong with the media company. In a world where brand recognition and rights ownership are the twin goals for media companies, it would appear Pearson has plenty of both; the *Financial Times*, Penguin Books, Thames Television, Madame Tussauds – even a stake in Channel 5 – are just a few items in the company's extensive portfolio. Yet the City has become increasingly exasperated with the company's underperformance. In 1995 it turned over £1.8bn, but made only £235.7m. in profit – partly because of management misadventures. The £313m. purchase of the clearly overrated Californian multimedia company Mindscape was a particular howler – it lost £47m. last year.

An amateur atmosphere pervades the Pearson board: the involvement of the Cowdray family, which still has a significant interest in the company, and the chairmanship of Lord Blakenham made the company appear more county than City to some outsiders. This is perhaps an unfair accusation, as the outgoing chief executive Frank Barlow has tenacious industrial credentials.

The 1993 decision to turn Pearson from a conglomerate to a media company meant the sale of companies as diverse as oil services and Royal Doulton china. But the ensuing acquisition of, seemingly, anything for sale – Hong Kong television companies, American publishers, Mindscape – showed little discernment. Even plans to sell the company foundered as predators scoured the balance sheet to find that the business was already very fully valued.

"They have excellent brands that should turn in a premium profit but, unfortunately their track record does not match this expectation," says David Forster, media analyst at Salomon Brothers.

What should Scardino and the new chairman, Denis Stevenson, do to make Pearson a media contender? Everyone you ask says the same: "focus", "focus" and "focus".

Analyst Meg Geldens of Merrill Lynch says: "There should not be too much short-term pressure on them to do anything drastic but, over time, it is clear that Pearson needs to decide what it wants to be a market leader in and really concentrate on that area." She points to the experience of Reed Elsevier, the Anglo-Dutch publisher, which has stripped out much of its consumer activity to focus on business and educational information services.

The obvious candidates for disposal on this count must be Madame Tussauds and Lazards, the banking concern. Confident predictions have already been made that the latter will buy back its own shares from Pearson in order to gain independence, although others say the group would be short-sighted to dump a cash-generating business for the sake of tidiness. Tussauds and interests in Spanish theme parks also stand out as leisure rather than content businesses.

The overriding question, however, is what will happen to the company's TV interests. Pearson TV comprises Thames Television, producer of *The Bill*, *Minder* and *Neighbours*, alongside gameshow originator Reg Grundy, a small residual stake in BSkyB, a further stake in satellite operator SES and a 20 per cent share of Channel 5. Although Scardino might find her aims and approach more attuned to those of Greg Dyke, head of Pearson TV, than many of the Pearson executives, it could be in both Dyke's and Scardino's interests for the company to be cut loose.

What would Pearson be left with if it took this route? Mainly, its publishing names. Acquisitions made at the end of 1996 must have had at least the blessing of Scardino and Stevenson, if not their direct involvement. The purchase of South African newspapers followed by that of the American publishing house Putnam indicate that Pearson may be thinking of sticking to its print roots and ditching the glitz of broadcasting.

Pearson's mistake was to fall for the fantasy that cross-media ownership is a sound strategy. As Salomon's Forster says: "*The Bill* really has nothing to do with the *Financial Times* or a wax museum." The shimmering promise of synergies between paperbacks, television rights and CD-Rom – one piece of content across all formats – has so far flopped for Pearson and, indeed, other practitioners of the cross-media position. The truly successful media companies of the 1990s are proving to be those with a dogged focus and a determination to lead their market or maintain excellence in one area – even if it makes them as crushingly dull as Reuters or Reed. As one industry observer put it, "When was the last time Ted Turner bought a newspaper?" If Pearson concentrated on one type of information or one sort of entertainment across a narrower range of formats, it might have more success.

(Source: *Observer*, 12 January 1997.)

from rival firms. In this emergent phase there are no "rules of the game" established, which means that a wide variety of products are on offer made by many different processes, and some firms are advertising heavily, while others are relying on their access to distribution channels to push the product into the market place. Often market share gained in the early stages of an industry's development can reap rich rewards later on, especially if there are advantages to be gained from acquiring experience faster than the competition (the experience curve effect). However, this assumes that the basis of competition remains the same. If it changes – for instance, from a strong emphasis on manufacturing experience to keep costs down, to a new emphasis on the importance of marketing sophistication – these advantages are considerably reduced.

As the industry starts to mature, "rules" become accepted and understood, consumers now have expectations about quality and performance, and industry standards are established. Competition, in the transition to maturity, will become more intense as rapid growth can now only be achieved by capturing customers from rival firms. Cumulative experience no longer provides an important advantage to one firm because all firms have now gained all the advantages that are available. A significant feature of maturing industries is the tendency for competition to be based on price, since firms' product offerings tend to become very similar and attempts at innovation are soon copied.

In declining industries, only the most efficient firms can earn reasonable profits, and the marginal players are "shaken out" of the industry. Where there are high exit barriers, rivalry can become very intense as marginal firms hang on in the industry, leading to chronic overcapacity.

Interrelationships between the five forces

We need to understand how a change in one of the five forces can impact upon another. Let us suppose that, due to a technological breakthrough, entry into the industry became much easier. If the industry is earning above average profits, new firms are likely to enter. This in turn could make rivalry more intense, and may well feed through to the buyers, who are now better able to play one firm off against another.

So all these forces are interconnected, and changes in one are likely to impact on the others.

How can we forecast these changes?

Forecasting is notoriously difficult, but that is no reason not to try to think about the future. One way in to the problem is to look at *trends* in the environment that look as if they might continue into the future. The wider environment in which the firm and its industry is located can be subdivided for forecasting purposes into the following four sectors:

1. The **P**olitical environment.

2. The **E**conomic environment.

3. The **S**ocial environment.

4. The **T**echnological environment.

PEST analysis can be useful if it encourages us to think more broadly about environmental influences on the firm. Some examples of trends and changes in the wider environment are given in Figure 4.2.

Illustration 4.4 considers how the introduction of European monetary union might impact upon firms trading in Europe. The introduction of a single currency is clearly going to affect most businesses. The problem facing a particular firm is to try to work out more specifically how it will affect their operations and strategy. The check list included in the illustration should be applied to your firm's circumstances. One way of translating these broader issues into more precise understandings of how it might impact upon a particular firm is to use the five-forces model as a "filter" between the broader macroeconomic changes and the particular circumstances facing the firm. Thus the issues raised by the article in the illustration could be applied to each of the five forces in turn. For example:

◆ How will a single currency affect the way firms compete in our existing markets?

◆ Will it make entry into the market more or less easy?

◆ How will monetary union affect our customers' buying behaviour? Will it increase or decrease their power?

**Which environmental factors are the most important
at the present time, or will be in the next few years?**

Economic factors

Business cycles
GNP trends
Interest rates
Money supply
Inflation
Unemployment
Disposable income
Energy, availability and cost
Trade cycles

Technology

Government spending
   on research
Government and industry
   focus on technological effort
New discoveries/development
Speed of technology transfer
Rates of obsolescence

Sociocultural factors

Population demographics
Income distribution
Social mobility
Life-style changes
Attitudes to work and leisure
Consumerism
Levels of education

Political/legal

Monopolies legislation
Environmental protection laws
Taxation policy
(Foreign) trade regulations
Employment law
Government stability

The markets

Market size and trends
Market shares (by market
   segment)
Change in customer
   expectations/usage
Price/volume relationships

Figure 4.2 *Examples of trends and changes in the wider environment*

◆   How will it affect relationships with suppliers?

Why do all this analysis and why bother to speculate about an uncertain
future? Because, if you understand about the competitive dynamics of
your industry, you can then think about how to change things, or how
to manoeuvre the organization in to an optimum position to deal with
the threats and take up the opportunities that may be emerging.

Either the firm can adapt to the changing conditions, or the firm can
act to change the forces of competition. ''Forewarned is forearmed'': if

Illustration

4.4 EMU will bring opportunities and threats: companies must plan carefully

Companies across Europe have been promised many benefits from European economic and monetary union. The single currency is meant to provide lower interest rates and more competitive economies. It is also meant to encourage better integration of national markets, simplified financial management and elimination of exchange transaction costs.

However, EMU carries with it significant risks for companies, and will require intensive preparation across all aspects of business activity.

Companies can choose whether to make the minimum preparations necessary for EMU – or whether in addition to work to obtain advantages from the market changes which will follow. But ignoring EMU, and, in particular, ignoring the systems implications, is not an option.

Companies should define:

◆ their future vision of how they would operate in a euro environment;

◆ the opportunities and threats for each of their lines of business and countries of operation; and,

◆ very importantly, how they would handle the transition phase.

Time is now short before the introduction of the "paper" euro in 1999 and senior management should make EMU preparation a priority in the short term to ensure that companies can cope with the euro.

Among issues to be considered by companies are:

◆ *Marketing and pricing* Assess each of your markets to identify the way in which they will operate after the single currency is introduced: the euro will bring existing national markets closer together and in some industries will result in market restructuring. Review your pricing strategy, because it may not be possible to maintain price differentials between existing national markets. Consider how your competitors will react to the single currency: will they rationalize their operations? Work with your customers to agree a switch to euro purchasing and your switch to euro pricing. Find out when your suppliers wish to change to euro pricing.

◆ *Systems and IT* Identify the operational systems to be changed to deal with the euro. You will need to assess each operational system and decide which to modify, and assess the risks of systems failure to your business.

◆ *Finance and payroll* Decide when to change over your internal accounting to the euro. Decide when to change your payroll to euro (this is likely to be a year 2002 issue when coins and notes are available for retail use). Consider if your accounting will be affected by gains and losses between euro currencies which could crystallize in 1999.

◆ *Treasury and banking* Consider rationalizing your banking relationships in the euro area (you may need only one bank for euro payments). Identify savings by the reduction of treasury operations, or by setting up some form of joint service organization for euro invoicing.

◆ *Legal issues* Investigate contract continuity, particularly outside the EU where the EU regulations confirming contract continuity may not apply. Consider changes to your staff employment contracts and pension arrangements. Review contract terms and conditions to see that the euro is adequately covered.

◆ *Longer term* Review your operations to consider the advantages and threats of a single currency. For example, the existence of a large single currency area may lead you to consider relocating some operations there to avoid currency fluctuations.

(Source: *Financial Times*, 28 May 1997.)

your firm is thinking about the future rather more than the competition, you may be able to anticipate developments that may leave the competition reacting to, rather than controlling, events.

Competitor analysis

The market or "industry" environment is obviously key to the identification of opportunities and constraints facing the firm. However, for accurate competitive positioning, a more detailed and specific analysis of the "rivalry" category of the five-forces analysis needs to be carried out by means of an accurate profile of each of the firm's main competitors.

It is important to understand your competitors for the following reasons:

1. To try to predict their *future strategies*.

2. To assess accurately their probable *reactions to your strategic moves*.

3. To estimate their ability to *match* you in the quest for competitive advantage.

Competitor analysis is more important in some industry structures than in others. In terms of five-force analysis, the stronger the "rivalry" force, the more important it is to understand your rivals, since only then can you combat them successfully. In very fragmented industries, like hairdressing, for example, competitor analysis may not be crucial to success. Firms are typically small, the product or service may well be undifferentiated, and the key to success may be not a distinctive competitive strategy, but the provision of a valued service at an acceptable price to a number of locally semi-captive clients. Or the product may be a commodity (e.g. concrete), and price at the required quality is the only thing that matters in the buying transaction.

In a concentrated industry, however, competitor analysis is important, since the competitive battle is essentially between a small number of relatively large companies, normally with differentiated products, and often with strong brand names. In such cases, relative market share becomes crucially important in order to be able to keep down costs by taking advantage of the experience curve, of scale economies, and of scope economies as described in Chapter 3.

Competitor analysis is concerned with the following five basic attributes of the competitor:

1. Its comparative *market strength*.

2. Its *resources* and *core competences*.

3. Its current and possible *future strategy*.

4. Its *culture*, and hence the assumptions it makes about itself and the industry.

5. Its *objectives* and *goals*, both at corporate level and at business-unit level.

Competitor analysis must carried out on a segment-by-segment basis. In this way, the specific competences necessary to achieve competitive advantage in each segment are compared firm by firm.

The current strategy of competitors is discernible partly from what each company has to say, but more importantly from what it does. To assess either factor, a positive effort will need to be made at competitor data collection, in excess of the information that will easily come the company's way through a conscientious reading of the press. Effective competitor analysis requires the creation of a file on each competitor, which must be maintained in up-to-date condition by an enthusiastic executive who can act as "champion" for the specific task. In the absence as such conditions, the file is likely to become outdated after a few months.

The competitor's intended – or at least declared – strategy can usually be discovered from the chairman's message to shareholders in annual reports, and by interviews in the press given by senior executives. The competitor's *realized* strategy, however, is the more important, and this can only be discovered by tracking the competitor's actions over a period of time and by scanning it for consistency of purpose. Such direct observation can be supplemented by deliberately seeking out comments from suppliers who deal with both the analyst company and the competition, by interviewing buyers, by recruiting and debriefing executives from competitor companies, and by talking to journalists and other industry analysts. It is particularly important to gain early infor-mation of a competitor's possible change of strategy, and this may be signalled in a number of ways: by comment, by an unusual acquisition, by announced personnel changes at the top, and so forth.

The competitor's culture is normally an important factor in setting limits to the actions the competitor is likely to take in a market. An understanding of that culture will reveal the way the company operates, and the constraints within which it often *subconsciously* operates. A company's culture embodies the core values that executives in the company take for granted, and an understanding of that culture can therefore be very valuable to a competitor. In Chapter 6 we explore organizational culture in more depth.

The objectives of the competitors are a fifth factor to be assessed in a competitor analysis exercise. A company concerned to achieve short-term financial objectives, for example, is likely to react quite differently from one with longer-term market-share objectives and willing to take perhaps a ten-year view to establish its position in the market.

If the competitor is a subsidiary of a major corporation, it is also necessary to understand the basic objectives of the parent. A company owned by the Hanson Group, for example, will probably be far more constrained in terms of research and development expenditure, or in adopting a new initiative with a long gestation time, than would a company that is part of Shell, accustomed as the latter is to the high risks associated with oil exploration. The level of autonomy the competitor possesses in seeking to achieve its objectives is also relevant to the competitor assessment exercise.

Equipped with competitor information, the analyst will be in a strong position to address key questions, as follows:

1. Is the competitor satisfied with its current market position, or is it likely to become aggressive in the near future?

2. Where is the competitor most vulnerable?

3. Is it likely to change strategy in the near future? If so, how?

4. What action by us is likely to provoke the greatest/least retaliation by the competitors?

5. In what areas might it be possible to cooperate with the competitors?

6. How might we shift the basis of competition in the market towards qualities in which we have excellence?

It is based on answers to questions such as these that new ideas for achieving competitive advantage may be developed.

So what?

At the start of this chapter we suggested that there were two basic issues that segment-level analysis has to address:

1. *The nature of the effective demand* What is the nature of this demand in the segment? What are the needs of customers? What is the volume of demand? Is demand growing or shrinking?

2. *Competence imitability* How easy is it for firms to replicate the key competences required to meet the demand?

Having explained three techniques, we are now in a position to assess how useful they might be in addressing these issues. The first point to note is that all three techniques are essentially driven from a producer perspective. The focus is firmly on the firm (competitor analysis) or groups of firms (five-forces analysis). The main problem with this perspective is that it might not be an appropriate way to analyze a segment of demand, which is clearly a customer-driven perspective. As we explained earlier, mistakes can be made in the identification of who the real competitors might be if an overly producer-driven approach is adopted. Do Pizza Hut compete with other Pizza restaurants, or do they compete with McDonalds, Burger King, and so on. I believe that the most appropriate definition of a firm's competitors is the *customer's* definition, which may be quite different from that assumed by the management of the firm.

Some recent research has indicated that managers within a firm may hold significantly different views about whom their firm competes with – and again, these views can be quite different from those of other firms seemingly in the same "industry". Clearly, as far as competitive strategy is concerned, forging some real understanding of whom we actually compete with is crucial, and I would argue that the safest approach to defining competitors is to work back from customers and their views of which organizations offer them alternative ways of meeting their needs.

None of the three techniques described above shed much light on the nature and strength of demand. The five-forces technique perhaps comes closest in that it includes buyers and buyer power in its framework. In order to gain some deeper insights into segment demand, market research has to be undertaken. Commissioning market research can be expensive, particularly if the management have not clearly thought through the questions they want answers to. Often the quantitative data that is routinely collected is not particularly helpful, as it tends to be too aggregated to provide much of an insight into the nature of demand at segment level. The size of the segment can be fairly readily estimated if product sales information can be accessed, but again this can be frustrated where defining a segment in terms of products is not really appropriate.

To gain some deeper understanding of customers' needs, purchase motivations, and their perceptions of products on offer, the most appropriate technique is the focus group. Focus groups involve a small group of existing or potential customers coming together with a skilled researcher to talk about products, and also about their needs. This technique is superior to questionnaire-based research in probing for more subtle motivations and perceptions.

The three techniques considered in this chapter do, however, offer more assistance in addressing the second issue: imitability of competences. The five-forces framework addresses this issue explicitly when it considers "barriers to entry". Competitor analysis should also help in the identification of firms who may have the core competences to compete in a particular segment.

Overall, these three techniques can play a useful role in forcing a management team to address issues and questions that are not routinely discussed. The techniques can be adapted to suit differing environments. For example, I have used the five-forces framework with management teams from public sector organizations (e.g. government departments). Here "buyers" may not be the recipients of the service (i.e. the clientele of a public hospital), and it can therefore be more useful to think of the buyers as the politicians and influential civil servants who determine budget allocations to the organization.

Finally, given the time pressures most of us face, there may not be sufficient energy or will available to carry out all this analysis. If you have limited resources, don't squander them. If it is a choice between analyzing customers through the customer matrix, or analyzing competitors in great depth, go for the customers every time. Although we need to keep a weather eye on our closer competitors, the best way to deal with them is to give superior value for money to customers.

Summary

There are two critical issues at segment level: the nature of the effective demand in the segment, and competence imitability. We then explored three commonly used analytical approaches – the structural analysis of industries, competitor analysis, and PEST analysis – to assess the extent to which these techniques can help us answer questions of demand and imitability.

We concluded that these techniques were helpful, although they did not address our two concerns of demand and imitability in particularly direct ways. Their main benefit would appear to be in structuring and broadening strategic discussions, and in prompting managers to try to gather better quality information on their competitors.

CHAPTER 5

Strategy, structure and processes

Introduction

So far we have explored the firm's competitive positioning in the various markets within which it aims to compete. Issues of imitability have been raised in terms of helping the firm *sustain* a position of advantage. A relatively neglected area in competitive strategy is the link between product/market strategy and the structure of the firm. I believe that imaginative approaches to organizational structure can help a firm both gain and sustain advantage. In this chapter, therefore, we shall address the relationships between strategy, structure and organizational processes.

We shall approach this difficult area by starting with some very basic concepts: specialization and coordination, and then go on to consider the most typical organizational structure, the functional organization. The rest of the chapter is taken up with the development of a "contingency" approach to the strategy–structure relationship. This approach argues that there is no 'one best way' to structure an organization; it all depends on the situation facing the firm. Is it large or small? Is it facing a rapidly changing environment or a stable one? Does it have a huge range of products selling into many different markets, or is it basically a one-product firm? In order to determine the appropriate organizational structure to suit a particular strategy we need to identify the key variables that influence structure and the range of structural options available that fit particular combinations of these key contingency variables

Organizational structure: some basic concepts

The approach to structure summarized in this section is based on the work of Henry Mintzberg. Because, generally, managers appear to have

98

a rather undeveloped understanding of organization structure, I think that a sound grasp of some basic issues and themes will help to lift the level of debate. So, no apologies for taking a rather theoretical stance on structure. Stay with it, since mastering these concepts should really advance your understanding of structure.

The strategy–structure relationship addresses the following two issues:

1. Once the strategy has been decided, how should we carve up the overall tasks facing the firm into discrete activities, and how should we allocate them to individuals and groups – in essence, how should we *specialize*?

2. Having divided the task into manageable areas of activity, how do we make sure that it all gets done, so that the strategy is achieved – that is, how do we *coordinate* the separate activities?

The first issue, specialization, is reflected in the organizational structure of the firm: the departments or divisions that focus on particular activities. This is "horizontal" specialization. The different *levels* of management we refer to as "vertical" specialization. We can obtain a picture of the way the firm has chosen to specialize by inspecting its organization chart (see Figure 5.1). The most basic form of specialization is by *function*, which is explored in the next section. Staff can also be grouped in other ways: by product or product group, by type of customer, by

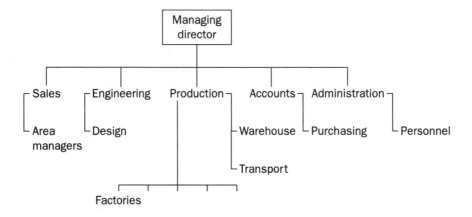

Figure 5.1 *A functional organization*

market or geography, or by project. There are advantages to grouping in particular ways as it helps to focus the development of expertise, and it facilitates the sharing of knowledge. However, specializing and grouping people around, for example, a project can lead to a gradual reduction in particular functional competences that are combined to deliver the project. This can happen because specialist engineers spend little time with other engineering colleagues, which reduces the flow of ideas and experience between these specialists. So each way of specializing has advantages and some disadvantages.

The second issue, coordination, is achieved through *organizational processes* that are designed to ensure that the separate activities are linked together in such a way that the overall mission of the firm is achieved. Six basic ways of achieving coordination can be identified, as follows:

1. *Direct, face-to-face discussion and communication* That is, between those engaged in different activities. This has been called "mutual adjustment". It can be a purely informal activity assisted by locating people in close proximity, or it can be facilitated by setting up formal meetings, project teams or task forces. The advantages of this coordinating mechanism are that it can help to achieve rapid changes to the way things are done, and it can encourage creativity by bringing together different specialists to work on a problem. The disadvantages are that it might be an ad hoc process leading to poor coordination, it can be time-consuming if extensive consultations are required, and it is not appropriate if large numbers of people are involved.

2. *Direct supervision* Here instructions about how to do parts of the overall task are issued by the manager to subordinates, and as long as the staff carry out their instructions the overall task is accomplished. This coordinating mechanism requires the manager to be able to understand the task, break it down into separate activities, and issue clear instructions to subordinates. Therefore, this mechanism is only really appropriate when fairly simple, easily understood tasks are being tackled. There is a limit to the number of subordinates that can be supervised in this management-intensive way, so the size of the organization and/or the size of each unit may

be constrained if this is the predominant coordinating mechanism to be employed. The main advantage of the approach is that rapid changes in activity can be achieved by the manager issuing different instructions.

3. *Standardizing the way the activities are performed* If an activity is to be repeated many times, it is worth finding out the best way of doing it. This is what method study tries to do. By standardizing the way the work is done, and by ensuring that one activity dovetails into the next step in the process, highly specialized activities can be effectively coordinated. This mechanism is only really applicable if the firm is facing a sufficiently predictable workload to justify the investment in standardization. Its advantage is that the work can be routinized to the point where semi-skilled or unskilled people can do it. The experience curve explained in Chapter 3 is largely based on the development of standardized "best practice". Its disadvantages emerge from the intrinsically boring and unchallenging work that may be an outcome of standardization, and the lack of organizational flexibility that may result. The organization is only really good at doing a limited range of tasks very efficiently.

4. *Standardization of outputs* Coordination between different activities can be achieved if, at each stage of the process, the activity produces a standardized output. This then becomes a standardized *input* for the next stage of production. Using tight specifications to set output standards can permit different activities to be performed in different locations (e.g. the coordination between the partners in Airbus Industries) or even in different organizations, through subcontracting.

5. *Standardization of skills* Here the people carrying out the activity have standardized skills. If they exercise their skills in the appropriate ways, their activities will mesh with the work of other specialists to enable the whole task to be accomplished. Organizations that use this mechanism extensively are "professional" organizations like accountancy practices, hospitals and universities.

6. *Standardization of values* This might seem a strange way of bringing about coordination. It refers to groups of people who

subscribe to a set of shared values that help to ensure they behave in predictable and appropriate ways. This form of coordination is particularly appropriate where the work of the organization is fragmented, and where staff inculcated with the right values can be trusted to perform in the "correct" way. Examples might be the army, police work, or, from the commercial sector, IBM or McDonalds. Standardization of values is made easier through selection processes that identify people with attitudes and beliefs which are similar to those required. However, the processes whereby people acquire and change their values are not well understood, and it may be extremely difficult to encourage a significant shift in the values held by a group of people. This is considered further in the next chapter.

Coordination within a particular organization can be achieved by using some, or possibly all of these mechanisms. However, one of the six mechanisms often tends to predominate, for example direct supervision, and can have a strong influence on the type of organization that emerges. For instance, where there is extensive use of work-process standardization, the organization tends to look like a "machine bureau-cracy" with a mass-production type of operations system, a large number of technical staff (production engineers, cost estimators, pro-curement, production scheduling and control, work measurement) and usually a rather heavy management presence, with many levels in the hierarchy and a fairly autocratic style.

As organizations grow, the predominant coordinating mechanism may change. For example, in a newly established small business, coor-dination is likely to be achieved either by direct supervision – the entrepreneur directs the activities of a few staff – or by face-to-face communication. These informal mechanisms are likely to be less effect-ive as the business grows: there are now too many people to supervise directly and informal communications are not sufficient to keep every-one in the picture. If the organization settles down into providing a limited range of products or services, it may be worth trying to standardize the way the products are made in order to improve productivity and quality: that is, to benefit from the advantages of the experience curve. If the organization subsequently diversifies into several lines of business, for example through acquisition, the corporate centre may choose to manage each business unit by setting profit targets, a form of output standardization.

The five parts of the organization

Mintzberg argues that an organization can be subdivided into five different parts, as follows:

1. *The strategic apex* These people control the organization and are held accountable for its performance.

2. *The operating core* These deliver the basic mission or task of the organization.

3. *The middle line* These are the managers and supervisors in direct line authority from the strategic apex to the operating core.

4. *The technostructure* These are staff analysts that help to bring about coordination through standardizing processes, outputs, skills or values.

5. *The support staff* These are staff activities that support the main work of the organization. For instance, in a manufacturing firm, support staff would include building maintenance, restaurant staff, public relations, office cleaning, and so forth.

The size and significance of these groups will vary depending on, for example, the type of work the organzation is doing, the stability of its environment, and the size of the organization. We therefore need to understand these "contingency variables" and the effect they have on the structure of the business. But before we explore these relationships, we shall refer briefly to the organizational processes that bring the structure to life.

Organizational processes

This chapter is concerned with the links between strategy, organization structures and organizational processes. Included in organizational processes are decision-making, delegation, formal and informal communication, training, indoctrination, quality assurance, operations planning and control, leadership, formal and informal power relationships, management information systems, budgetary control, target-setting, incentive systems and disciplinary procedures. The aim of these processes is either specialization (e.g. training) or coordination (e.g. quality control, planning, delegation, target-setting).

Certain types of structure make extensive use of particular processes. For example, operations planning and control, training, quality assurance and disciplinary processes are features of the large mass-production firm, the "machine organization". In contrast, informal communication networks, incentive systems and decentralized decision-making might be typically found in a software development company, the "innovative organization". Therefore, it is important to understand the role that organizational processes are playing in bringing about specialization or coordination within a particular organizational configuration, and not to view them as separate dimensions that can be changed or manipulated independently. Hence programmes that concentrate on changing quality systems or improving communications need to be tackled with a full appreciation of the role these processes play in the wider organization. Other aspects of formal and informal organizational processes are explored in more depth in the next chapter.

Linking strategy, structure and process

We shall now look at the links between strategy and structure. As most business units adopt some form of functional structure it is worth looking at the strategy–structure relationship within a functional structure first. We will then explore other strategy–structure relationships.

The functional structure

Most firms solve the first problem of organization, how we should specialize, by adopting a functional structure, which groups people according to the type of activity they are engaged in. An engineering organization might have the following functions: production, engineering, sales, accounts, administration, personnel, warehouse/transport (see Figure 5.1).

As a firm grows, the number of functional specializations tends to increase, and they may emerge in a typical order. For example, the very small one- or two-person firm concentrates initially on some form of *production* (e.g. making novelty candles). Growth in orders means that they have to think about how to manage the production activity, so more staff are taken on and some further specialization takes place within the production function: mould making, dying, finishing, packing. Managing the finances and accounts soon becomes an issue. Handled initially by a subcontractor, the firm's accountant, the volume of work now requires the employment of a full-time specialist *management accountant*. Initially, orders came in without the need for a great deal of marketing effort, but there may now be a need to employ *sales people*. The amount of paperwork increases, and the loss of a valuable order through poor administration leads to the development of systems to handle orders, cash flow, scheduling and so on.

Thus, as the firm grows, activities that initially formed just part of the founder's responsibility emerge as specializations in their own right, and within functions, further specialization takes place.

Coordination within the operational area in a larger firm is probably achieved through standardization of work processes. The way the work is done is decided by, for example, work study or production engineers, and coordination across the functions is probably achieved through a combination of direct supervision (decisions and interventions by the managing director), standardization (budgets and targets will be set for each function) and ad hoc discussion or formalized meetings between managers from different functions (mutual adjustment).

Functional specialization has the advantage of encouraging the development of expertise, but the downside is that it can lead to parochialism and poor coordination of activities across the organization. It is probable that some form of functional specialization is essential in most organizations, otherwise the basic tasks of the organization could not be fulfilled effectively: for example, patients treated, newspapers printed, cars designed and manufactured. These basic tasks are likely to be common to all firms in a particular industry.

Most organizations display some form of functional specialization. However, the extent and type of specialization varies between organizations, and the predominant coordination mechanisms vary as well. We

now set out a contingency approach to the strategy–structure relationship that can be used to explore these variations in structural form.

A "contingency" approach to strategy and structure

Nowadays, few writers would subscribe to the classical rules of good
organization (e.g. "unity of command", limited "span of control"),
favouring instead a *contingency* approach. This approach takes as its
starting point that there is no one best way to organize – it all depends
on the situation. The most thorough exposition of the contingency
approach is probably Mintzberg's synthesis of prior studies in organization set out in his *Structuring of Organizations* (Prentice Hall, 1979). He
argues that the appropriate organizational form is contingent upon the
states of certain variables: the *age* of the organization, its *size*, *environmental dynamism* and *complexity*, external *power* relationships, and the
technical system employed by the organization: for example, small batch
production, or continuous flow processes.

Particular combinations of these contingent variables would indicate
that some organizational forms are more appropriate than others. For
example, a "machine bureaucratic" structure would fit the following
set of contingency conditions: a stable environment, a simple task,
powerful external influences, and the old and large organization.

Strategy as such is not referred to explicitly in Mintzberg's contingency approach. We could infer, however, that insofar as a strategy
determines, for instance, a firm's target markets, how it is to address its
environment (i.e. to compete on price and become the lowest-cost
producer), the contingent variables identified by Mintzberg would, *inter
alia*, be determined by the strategy. In other words, we are aiming to
serve an essentially stable environment, we must achieve large volumes
to be the lowest-cost producer, the chosen technology is a regulating
mass production system, and so on. This relationship could be set out as
follows:

strategy → contingent variables → structure

Mintzberg suggests that, although in theory there is a potentially huge
array of organizational forms, in reality just a few configurations
account for most types of organization. He identifies the *machine* organization, the *professional* organization, the *entrepreneurial* organization, the

diversified organization, the *innovative* organization, and the *missionary* organization. The fact that commonly occurring structures can be found amongst firms in the same industry lends some support to the configuration argument. If firms face the same contingent conditions, then a process of natural selection would drive them to take on the same structural form. I think this would be true where firms are being compared in fairly broad terms, but, as we saw in Chapter 3, sources of advantage can derive from quite subtle differences in the way common activities are performed in different firms. Embedded know-how may be present in one firm and lacking in another, even though their structures, on the face of it, look very similar. Thus, within the broad arguments advanced by the contingency approach, we should also be alert to more "fine-grained" differences at the operational and tactical level that can confer advantage.

Changes in the contingent variables

If the strategy of the organization leads to *significant* changes in the contingent variables, substantial structural changes may be required, which may result in the firm moving from one configuration to another: for example, from a machine organization to a divisionalized structure. These *interstructural* changes may be required in the following circumstances:

◆ When substantial changes in *product/market scope* have been introduced: new markets, exporting, launching different types of product in existing markets, diversification, new products and new markets.

◆ When there have been significant shifts in the *tasks* facing the firm: the tasks may have become increasingly complex, or technical or procedural developments may have simplified the task.

◆ When there have been significant changes in the *dynamism of the environment*: an increased pace of change in the unpredictability of the environment requires the firm to be much more flexible and adaptable.

◆ When the "*rules of the game*" have been changed: increasing competitive pressures lead to more emphasis being given to, for example, the pace of new product introductions, the tight control of costs, moves towards vertical integration (either forwards into distribution or retail, or backwards into component manufacture), increasing use of subcontractors for core activities.

Changes of this nature and scope are likely to put the existing structure under considerable pressure. There is evidence to suggest that structural reorganization often lags well behind the change in strategy. There is an inertia in many organizations, compounded by a reluctance on the part of top management to grasp the nettle of structural change, that results in damaging mismatches being perpetuated between the new strategic position of the firm and the former, now inappropriate, structure. Unfortunately, it is often only when a crisis of some sort is reached that the necessary structural changes are introduced. The crisis may take the form of, for example, a dramatic downturn in performance, a takeover threat, or replacing the chief executive officer.

Illustration 5.1 explains how Unilever have approached their restructuring. The corporation's structure seemed to be inhibiting its ability to compete. The example also shows the links between structure and the processes of decision-making, performance measurement, capital allocation, and incentives. Time will tell whether the planned reorganization will solve Unilever's problems.

Strategy changes that result in significant changes in the contingency variables will require shifts in structure to achieve a better strategy–structure alignment. To explore the structural implications of changes in the contingent variables resulting from the strategy change we can refer to Figure 5.2, where three of the more important contingent variables are presented in the form of continuums. The organizational implications of each of these three contingent variables are expected to be as follows:

1. *Environmental dynamism* When the organization is facing a relatively stable and predictable environment, the four standardizing processes – work processes, skills, outputs, values – are viable coordinating mechanisms. These mechanisms are likely to lead to a high degree of specialization and the emergence of staff groups involved in effecting standardization: for example, those staff concerned with production engineering, organization and methods,

5.1 Unilever changes its formula

September 1 will be a historic day in the life of Unilever, the Anglo-Dutch consumer products leviathan whose vast portfolio of brands includes Persil, Birds Eye and Walls. On that date, the three-man special committee – British chairman, Dutch chairman and the chairman-designate – which has run the group since Unilever was formed will be dissolved. Its place will be taken by a seven-person executive committee, vanguard of the group's most fundamental organizational reformation for three decades.

The origin of Unilever's structural problems lay in the late 1980s, when its spectacular mid-decade growth began to flag.

The company is suffering by comparison with its peers – Procter & Gamble, Nestlé and L'Oréal. By last year, Unilever's non-executive directors were asking questions about performance drift. Despite recurrent rationalization charges, the company was showing classic signs of organization fatigue: lack of dynamism and an excess of bureaucracy. Its main distinguishing feature was confusion – of accountability, with second-guessing rife, and of responsibility. Head office had become a mish-mash of corporate, regional, coordinating and service duties. "Extra levels of complexity were imposed on an already convoluted structure," says Lang. "Increasingly, Unilever managers found themselves responsible to two or more masters. Often they were faced with conflicting priorities. Decision-making sometimes became constipated. Managers became frustrated and demotivated, not least because of the devaluation of operating company chairman status to which most aspired. At the top of the ladder, the move towards globalization meant that senior management was spending too much of its time at 40,000 feet."

When top executives were not in transit, they were being called on to make decisions that should have been sorted out much lower down the organization. Or they were in meetings. One observer says the diaries of senior managers had become so cluttered with committees, "you wondered when they had time to sleep. Presumably, they slept in the meetings."

Now Unilever has called a halt to this process of corporate self-absorption. The radical restructuring, being implemented under the banner, "Shaping for Outstanding Performance", will abolish the system of worldwide business coordinators. Below them, the network of regional directors will be swept away. These two layers will be replaced by a single team of fourteen business presidents, with operations grouped by product in Unilever's established regions of Europe and North America and in its industrial activities, and by region in the rest of the world. Executive committee members and group presidents will meet in a new executive council, which will become the company's supreme policy-making body. The extent of the shake-up is embodied in the fact that half the twenty-two members of the council are new appointments to senior posts, and only around half are British or Dutch.

Apart from streamlining and crystallizing Unilever's decision-making processes, the new structure represents an attempt to develop a truly global group by means that run counter to accepted multinational wisdom. Unilever intends to globalize by devolution, not centralization. While giving its executive committee total responsibility for overall strategic leadership, it is taking pains to devolve full operational responsibility, including regional strategy development, to the business group presidents.

As such, the new organization signals the end, so far as the group is concerned, of centrally driven expansion. The new Unilever will grow as much by local pull as by global push. It is setting out to turn its variegation, its innate diversity, into a source of competitive advantage. "We used to think of ourselves as a European business with interests in North America and outside," says one executive. "In the new organization, Europe is just another region and it has to justify its existence along with all the rest." With so much of world economic growth coming from Asia, that new equality should play a decisive part in restoring Unilever's flagging momentum.

The obvious danger in devolving so much freedom of action, however, is that the new centrifugal Unilever will spawn a number of regional baronies which create duplicate bureaucracies, wasting resources instead of liberating them. The end result would be fragmentation.

But powerful mechanisms are in place to prevent this and ensure that the regional groups use rather than abuse their new freedom. Each president will report directly to Tabaksblat and FitzGerald, the joint chairmen. The executive committee will be responsible for agreeing business plans with the fourteen groups, monitoring their implementation and intervening if the plans are not met: "not interfering, but intervening decisively if there is a major deviation from plan," says the "Outstanding Performance" document. The key interface between committee and presidents, between strategic direction and operating freedom, will be a new annual plan contract, with four components: strategic, investment, and human resource matters, and operational targets.

The drive for competitive advantage will be strengthened by a second major reform, introduced alongside the structural change. On 1 January, the company installed a new measure, trading contribution, which will form its fundamental yardstick for gauging its financial performance and enhancement of shareholder value. Lang says:

"We rate Unilever's fresh financial approach equal in importance to its new organizational structure in terms of its ability to change deep-rooted behavioural patterns. It represents a decisive shift to value management."

Trading contribution will form the base measurement of performance for each of the fourteen business groups, and will be the key criterion for determining bonus payments under a new management incentive system. The system is derived from the concept of Economic Value Added (EVA), now used by many leading US firms including Coca-Cola and AT&T to assess returns to shareholders. Like conventional performance measures, Unilever's trading contribution emphasizes growth, cash flow and business mix, being calculated on after-tax earnings with an adjustment for working capital inflation and replacement cost depreciation. Where it departs from the norm is in also taking account of capital efficiency, via a capital charge struck at 1 per cent above Unilever's estimated 6 per cent cost of equity capital. That also links the financial plan to the share price.

(Source: *Management Today*, July 1996.)

budgeting and standard costing, training and induction, and operations planning and control. Standardization becomes less viable when the organization is facing a rapidly changing and unpredictable environment. Increasing environmental dynamism can be coped with through flexible organization structures that encourage informal communication: matrix structures, project teams.

2. *Task complexity* When the basic tasks of the organization are straightforward those tasks can be broken down into easily understood activities. Simple tasks mean that decisions can be made centrally, using direct supervision as the coordinating mechanism, and when they are broken down into separate, simple steps, relatively unskilled people can carry them out. Complex tasks cannot be broken down into easily understood steps, and usually require highly skilled specialists to execute them. With complex tasks, decision-making tends to be located at the level of experts with the required specialist knowledge: task complexity then tends to be associated with decentralized decision-making.

3. *Product/market diversity* Firms trading in one market with a limited range of products can manage effectively with a

Environmental dynamism

• Pace of change; uncertainty

Lo   Hi

Bureaucratic   Organic
Specialization   Collaboration
Standardization   Adaptable

Task complexity

• One brain cannot cope; task cannot be broken down into easily understood subtasks

Lo   Hi

Centralization   Decentralization
Low task skills   High task skills

Product/market diversity

• Serving different markets; offering many different products

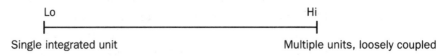

Lo   Hi

Single integrated unit   Multiple units, loosely coupled

Figure 5.2 *Main contingent variables*

single, integrated unit. As the markets served and/or the range of products offered become more diverse, the single unit is placed under strain. The requirements of different products and markets tend to pull the organization in different directions, leading to conflicting demands and priorities. If no structural change takes place the resulting performance of the firm is likely to deteriorate. Increasing diversity is best dealt with by allowing parts of the organization to tailor their activities to match the particular requirements of the product/markets they serve, leading ultimately to a multidivisional structure. One interim solution is the *matrix* structure, which usually involves overlaying the existing functional specializations with a product/market or project organization.

Combinations of these contingent variables lead to pressure to adopt particular types of structure. Four different combinations of task complexity and environmental dynamism are represented in Figure 5.3. Firms tackling simple tasks in stable environments are likely to evolve structures that are centralized and use extensive work-process standardization. As the environment becomes more dynamic, standardization becomes less viable, as the firm needs to be much more responsive to unpredictable changes. Because of the basic nature of the tasks, coordination can be effected through direction from the top.

Complex tasks being tackled in stable environments mean that it is worthwhile investing time in developing specialist skills to cope with the complexities involved (e.g. in surgery). Each specialist can work almost independently if the environment remains stable and predictable. The anaesthetist and the surgeon need not even speak to each

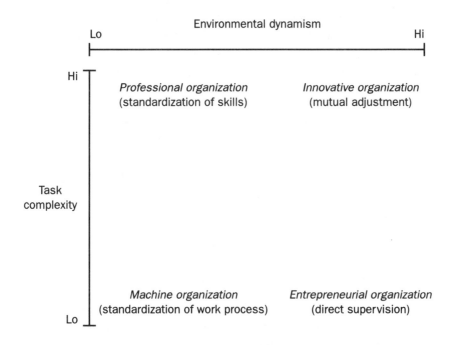

Figure 5.3 *Combinations of task complexity and environmental dynamism*

other in the operating theatre. However, increasing dynamism and unpredictability mean that new problems emerge, and new creative solutions are required. Now the experts must collaborate in multi-disciplinary teams that form and reform according to changing task demands.

Structural responses to changes in strategy and environment

Changes in the environment (e.g. from stable to dynamic) can be regarded as passive strategic decisions insofar as the firm's management chooses to continue to operate in the changing environment. They could, conceivably, consider withdrawing from increasingly hostile environments. However, changes in task complexity and product market diversity are more clearly the stuff of strategic decisions.

If the strategy change involves a shift along just one of the three main contingent variables it should be fairly clear what the required structural changes are likely to be. Moreover, coherent structures can be achieved with the four combinations of environmental dynamism and task complexity set out in Figure 5.3. Mintzberg in *Structures in Fives: Designing Effective Organisations* (Prentice Hall, 1983) identifies the four structure types as follows:

1. *Simple task/stable environment = the machine organization* A centralized bureaucracy with formalized procedures, sharp divisions of labour, functional groupings and an elaborate hierarchy; an extensive group of staff analysts concerned with effecting work standardization, and a large support staff to reduce uncertainty.

2. *Simple task/dynamic environment = the entrepreneurial organization* A simple structure, few staff roles and few middle managers; activities revolve around the founding entrepreneur, who coordinates through direct supervision.

3. *Complex task/stable environment = the professional organization* A large and powerful operating core consisting of highly specialized professionals (lawyers, surgeons, professors); a

large support staff, shallow hierarchy, with coordination being effected by standardization of skills.

4. *Complex task/dynamic environment = the innovative organization* An organization which typically has a fluid, organic and decentralized structure, experts deployed in multidisciplinary teams, coordination through mutual adjustment, and perhaps a matrix structure.

Each of these four configurations are internally consistent combinations of structure and organization processes that are suited to the tasks and environments facing them. However, because the systems, structures and processes are mutually consistent and reinforcing, changing from one configuration to another is very difficult. Each configuration exhibits its own self-preserving dynamic or momentum, which leads to the structure continuing long after the strategy or environment has changed. As suggested earlier, it is often only when the mismatch between the new strategy and the old structural arrangements becomes so great that performance dramatically deteriorates, that a structural reorganization is attempted.

The problems involved in shifting from one configuration to another are immense, particularly if the change challenges existing values and power structures. The move from one configuration to another is likely to be evolutionary in nature, and may even be only perceptible in hindsight.

Structural transformations that involve a shift in just one contingent variable are likely to be less challenging than those requiring shifts in two or three variables. For example, if the entrepreneurial organization is successful, growth in orders may reduce the unpredictability of the environment. The essentially simple nature of the tasks, coupled with increasing stability and an increasing volume of work, should lead to the firm effecting a smooth transition into the machine organization, as more parts of the task are standardized and routinized. This change would probably not seriously challenge the centralization of decision-making. However, the values of those who were involved in the early entrepreneurial years (resulting from shared experiences in overcoming the challenges of starting a new business) may well be quite different from those of new employees, who may have a more calculative involvement in the firm. They are there for the money.

5.2 **Altered states in the office**

Illustration

The call came while Linda Corbett was in her yard gardening. A supervisor at Pacific Bell wanted to know whether Ms Corbett would consider returning to the company from which, just six months earlier, she had been "severed involuntarily".

Ms Corbett, aged 42, resisted. She had reacted to her redundancy by plunging into suburban life. But she finally gave in, returning to a sales job at the company that had employed her since high school. However, instead of going back as an employee she returned as a contract worker, on the payroll of a temporary job agency. That contract workers are widely used is well known. What is coming to light is that as many as one-fifth of them are people like Ms Corbett who have returned to their old companies.

New surveys are beginning to document the trend, which appears to be another move toward a system in which companies and employees feel less obligated to one another.

"Many companies don't want to lose experienced people and they don't want to keep them on expensive career tracks," said Alan Krueger, a Princeton labour economist. "So they have come up with contract-worker status for ex-employees. And that is an important step that companies are taking towards rewriting the implicit contract that bound them to their workers. These former employees returning on contract become a subculture in the workplace. They are people with an employee's mindset spliced to an outsider's role. Some praise the liberation from enervating office politics, and from the stress of competing for pay rises and promotions. They talk of a greater flexibility to work when they please. But their altered status cuts at their self-esteem. Sometimes shunned by co-workers, they are often less effective. Many find themselves no longer going the extra mile to get a job done or acquire a skill.

Some come to realize, as Ms Corbett has, that what they have returned to are set tasks, rather than work that draws on their ingenuity. For many, company benefits like health insurance and pensions become only a memory. Corporations view these workers as skilled reserves who can jump back in without losing time learning a routine. But productivity suffers. The phenomenon of former employees cycling back to their companies as contract workers is still small, but if it spreads, says Mr Krueger, the economist, we come "that much closer to a world in which employment is no longer the primary source of pensions and health care, and we may have to choose other arrangements".

Ms McGuinness's $42,000 pension settlement is no match for what she would have received had she remained at Pacific Bell until retirement. And the company's health insurance expired six months after her job did. "I'll never get that back," she said. "My biggest heartache is what happened to my benefits."

(Source: *The Guardian*, Tuesday, 10 December 1996.)

Illustration 5.2 explains some of the effects of a particular form of structural change, moving from the employment of full-time employees to part-time staff. From the firm's point of view, the short-term cost advantages of laying off full-time staff need to be weighed against the longer-term effects on competitiveness. Sometimes, this rather crude form of cost-cutting destroys a source of advantage, like shared know-how, or a culture that encourages staff to contribute more than their contractual minimum effort.

If task complexity and environmental dynamism change, then the required shift from one configuration to another may be quite traumatic. Take, for example, a small management consultancy, with complex tasks in a dynamic environment (= innovative organization) that grows on the strength of a particular approach to payment systems. The firm begins to employ fewer skilled staff, using a proceduralized approach, increasing task simplification and environment stability, and leading inexorably towards the machine organization. The reasons why the founders started the venture – the pursuit of variety and autonomy, and the challenge of tackling complex problems – are replaced by the need to manage an increasingly centralized, bureaucratic organization.

Consider also the case of the manufacturing firm facing increasing foreign competition. Predictability in the environment is undermined, and in order to keep pace with competitive threats the firm needs rapidly to improve its products. So, the comfortable and stable situation that encouraged the emergence of a machine organization is replaced by an increasingly hostile and unpredictable environment and increasing task complexity as the pace of new product introductions is stepped up. These changes in contingent conditions could drive the firm towards the innovative organization, but this configuration is almost the polar opposite of the machine organization. Structures, processes, styles and values appropriate to one configuration are entirely inappropriate in the other, hence the challenge of managing such an organizational transformation are immense.

Coping with diversity

The strategic logic underpinning a move to increase product/market diversity must be considered when determining the appropriate structural response. For example, if the increasingly diverse product/market portfolio is the result of attempts to reduce the business risk of the corporation, then it would be appropriate to manage the activities involved in serving these product/markets in autonomous business units. However, if the increasing diversity is the outcome of a strategy built on the notion that the firm possesses some core capabilities, then structures and processes will be required that enable the corporation to utilize these skills across a widening scope of activities. Similarly, if the increasing diversity is the result of attempts to achieve synergy by bringing two businesses together, so that the whole is greater than the sum of the parts, then systems and structures will be required to foster the transfer of expertise, shared procurement, R & D and so on.

The strategic logic of the move towards increased product/market diversity is therefore central to decisions about the appropriate structural form to adopt. Here, the tensions and conflicts in strategy–structure relationships become apparent. Product/market diversity is best managed where subunits are allowed to develop activities that are tailored to particular product/markets. However, leveraging core skills across different subunits, sharing resources and centralizing certain activities (e.g. bulk purchasing) operate against the logic of the decentralized multiunit structure.

The benefits of fostering interrelationships between units and sharing resources need to be weighed against the advantages of subunit autonomy, tailoring activities and management accountability. Compromise solutions are possible where certain activities are managed centrally in order to gain the advantage of scale and scope economies (e.g. procurement of standard inputs, basic research), while preserving the essential autonomy and bottom-line accountability of each business unit. We explore these issues in more depth in Chapter 8.

Before we leave this exploration of strategy–structure relationships, we need to note that structure also has a strong role in *constraining* strategy. We shall take this issue up in the following chapter.

So what?

We conclude with the following set of practical implications of the arguments contained in this chapter:

- Structure is important, and it deserves serious consideration. Management teams should be encouraged to *challenge* the existing structure, and *explore* different ways of organizing.

- The structure of the organization sets out how the overall task facing the firm has been broken out into separate, specialized jobs. Looked at another way, the structure sets out responsibilities and accountabilities. These should be driven by the strategy of the firm. So if the strategy requires a focus on cost reduction, or more rapid new product introductions, or improved coordination with key suppliers, then someone should be responsible for these things. By allocating a clear responsibility to an individual, that person can be given the resources and authority to pursue that priority, and he or she can be held accountable for progress.

- Specialization allows people to become expert at one part of the task. To deliver value to customers, however, these separated activities must be coordinated together. So where you encourage specialization you must think clearly about how all these parts are to be linked back together. The simplest form of coordination is to encourage people to meet together. This can be facilitated by locating people in the same space, or by encouraging communication via electronic means (e.g. phones, E-mail, video conferencing).

- Structural changes tend to be avoided, but delay in realigning the structure merely builds up stresses that manifest themselves in poor performance. I suspect that many senior managers lack the confidence to tackle a major structural change, for fear of disrupting the basic *routines* of the organization. We explore routines further in the next chapter, and the issue of self-confidence is addressed in Chapter 7.

◆ All structural solutions, whether they be a straightforward functional organization, a matrix, or a divisionalized form, are a *compromise*. Functional structures are excellent at fostering expertise, but they create problems of coordination across the separated functional activities. Matrix structures address the problems of cross-functional integration, but at the cost of clarity in reporting arrangements and accountability. Divisionalized structures are designed to allow business units or divisions to focus on their particular markets, but this can hamper the achievement of synergies *across* these divisions. The trick is to adopt the structure which is most appropriate at delivering the primary thrust of the competitive strategy, and to address the weaknesses in the selected structure in other ways. Thus, for example, to be more customer focused we regroup people into teams to address different customer types (e.g. large corporate account, small businesses, personal customers), and we address the problems of sharing expertise across these customer-focused units by convening regular team meetings of, say, engineering staff located across the divisions.

◆ When a new CEO changes the structure of the organization, often the chosen solution is one that is well known to the CEO. This gives the CEO the confidence in the *detail* of the new structure; he or she is very familiar with the day-to-day routines, and understands how the organization should look and feel.

◆ As all structures are a compromise, most structures can be made to work if people want them to work. As soon as morale dips, however, all the ambiguities, tensions and problems within the structure will be exposed and exploited to meet the narrower sectional interests of individuals or groups.

Summary

Finally, this chapter has focused attention on major structural changes. However, although the same broad structures might be adopted by competing firms, they can contain subtle differences between firms at a more operational level, which can be the sources of competitive advantage. Chapter 3 highlighted the role of know-how and tacit knowledge in competitive advantage. In the following chapter we explore this phenomenon from the perspective of the *culture* of the organization.

CHAPTER 6

Strategy and culture

Introduction

A great deal of attention has been focused in strategy literature on the culture of organizations. In large part, this can be explained by the failure of the more "rational" approaches to strategy that were developed and propounded in the 1960s and 1970s. Corporate planning did not appear to be delivering the required strategic changes. Organizational culture, and the need to take account of it in strategic management, formed part of the explanation of the problems of strategy implementation.

Unfortunately, the term "culture" has been used to refer to almost every aspect of the organization, to the point where it might cease to be a useful concept. Probably the most accessible view of culture is summed up in the phrase, "*the way we do things around here*".

Organizations are likely to evolve different ways of tackling essentially the same tasks. For example, employees in a small regional accountancy firm that was taken over by one of the majors experienced substantial changes in the way they carried out essentially the same auditing tasks: the process was more formalized, senior staff were involved in planning the audit, set procedures had to be followed, reports and analyses had to be presented to the client in a standardized format. Illustration 6.1 briefly explains the culture of ICI, and how it both helped and hindered the corporation. The key issue at ICI was the enduring nature of the culture, which was able to withstand deliberate attempts to redirect the product/market strategies of the corporation.

Although, intuitively, the view of culture as "the way we do things" probably make sense, we need to delve a little deeper into this important aspect of organizations if we are to understand the role that culture plays in strategy. To assist in this exploration we shall first set out an overview of the role of culture in the strategy process, and then go on

6.1 Imperial Chemical Industries

In the mid-1960s, commentators were unable to mention Imperial
Chemical Industries without adding "Britain's biggest industrial
company". But today ICI ranks about thirtieth in the UK by market
capitalization, and trails, for example, BTR on almost every measure.
More to the point, ICI has lost touch with its three long-standing
German rivals, Hoechst, Bayer, and BASF, and has been overhauled by
Rhône-Poulenc of France. Once an industrial colossus, it is now just
another big chemical company.

There was a time when ICI could always be assured of the
minister's ear, and of a seat at the table. Before 1939, like Roman
triumvirs, Du Pont, ICI and the Germans had divided the world between
them. Cartels were out of favour post-war, but from their London
fortress at Millbank, ICI's rulers continued to control a huge portion of
the chemical industry of Britain's tottering Commonwealth. At the end
of the 1960s the company employed some 200,000 people spread
across eight UK divisions (plus one on the Continent) and 400
scattered subsidiaries. By head count, if by no other reckoning, ICI was
the world's greatest chemical company.

A vast bureaucracy served the rulers of this empire. Each division
had its head office close to a manufacturing centre, but Millstone
House – as it was known – determined strategy and allocated
resources. It also planned, coordinated, monitored and otherwise gave
support to a board whose structure, in the 1960s and 1970s, was
bizarre, unique and exceedingly British. The average ICI director had a
general oversight of one of the divisions (but was not profit-responsible),
kept an eye on the group's business in a far corner of the globe, and
looked after a staff function. In fact, he had wide-ranging powers
without personal responsibility. And when divisions had strong technical
or trading links, the relevant board members came together in "policy
groups" – creating potent cabals in the boardroom.

The baronies were exceedingly difficult to dislodge. After ICI's
humiliating (failed) bid for Courtaulds at the start of the 1960s, the
directors vowed that never again would a chairman achieve an
ascendancy like Sir Paul Chambers. Those who followed him were able
men who had risen through the hierarchy, and reached the head of the
table via an arcane process resembling that of the old Tory party.
(There was no vote: a senior board member would "take soundings"
and report to the retiring chairman who would name his own successor.)
ICI had no chief executive, and the chairman was explicitly "primus inter
pares". Thus no one had the capacity to initiate radical change.

The organization that evolved along with this regime was naturally
cumbersome. It was also (overlooking the Courtaulds affair) well

behaved. ICI was amply stocked with intelligent, educated and decent people, and its basic humanity was evident in, for example, its progressive personnel policies. But speed, agility and a sharp commercial instinct were not among its attributes. On occasion, decisions were made but nothing happened. At the start of the 1970s, the board agreed that the group should lower its exposure to bulk chemicals by investing more in high added-value specialities. However, the need to protect a market share in commodities meant that these operations developed a momentum of their own. When the directors took stock ten years later, the distribution of the business was virtually unchanged – and commodities were responsible for ICI's mounting problems.

A loss in 1980 was the first of a series of jolts that have shaken the group to its roots. The shock allowed Sir John Harvey-Jones to enlarge the chairman's powers and undermine the baronies. It lent new vigour to the drive for added value, and into overseas markets. Bulk products were lumped into a business-within-a-business – Chemicals & Polymers – making it simpler to hive them off some time.

Ironically, in 1993, it was the added-value bioscience businesses that were demerged, as Zeneca. The then chairman Sir Denys Henderson insists the split was conceived within ICI, although Lord Hanson's famous share stake undoubtedly had an influence. There has been no more talk of evolution. Change has caught up with ICI. Traces of the imperial past are still evident, but acquisitions, plant closures, joint ventures, asset swaps and new technologies have transformed the landscape. And the payroll is barely a quarter of its length of thirty years ago.

Henderson was not only chairman but chief executive. The present chairman, Sir Ronald Hampel, has a chief executive as his number two – Charles Miller Smith, recruited from outside ICI. In recent years, top management has learned to respect the shareholder. It's been a long journey from 1966 – and a long learning curve.

(Source: *Management Today*, May 1996.)

to explain the more important dimensions of culture. Finally, we shall explore the implications of culture on the strategic decision processes and on the processes of strategic change.

Culture and strategy

Figure 6.1 indicates a way in which the culture of the organization affects realized strategy. Processes within and outside the organization

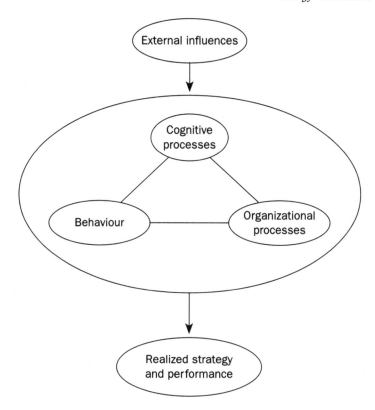

Figure 6.1 *How the culture of an organization affects strategy*

influence how people interpret and make sense of the world, and modify their individual perceptions and cognitions. Internal organizational processes include the formal and informal power relationships between individuals and groups, the control and reward systems, management style, and organization symbols. "External influences" is a catch-all term for all the sources of life experiences that shape an individual's view of the world. The term includes socialization processes experienced by the individual, including education, family, cultural influences (local, regional and national), and the individual's past work experiences. These complex influences combine to affect the way individuals think, which we have called the cognitive process.

Included in cognitive processes are the values, beliefs, attitudes and assumptions an individual holds, which are formed through past experiences. A key issue in strategy is the extent to which values, beliefs and assumptions are held in common by the members of an organization. This is because values and beliefs held by individuals influence their behaviour: for example, the decisions they make, the actions they perform. If there is a large degree of agreement amongst the members of the organization, then it is likely that they will behave and respond in similar ways. This factor can be enormously powerful and beneficial if the shared beliefs and values are in line with the intended strategy of the organization and if the intended strategy is appropriate. However, if a change in strategy requires certain behaviours that run counter to the prevailing beliefs, then this represents a serious barrier to strategy implementation. More worrying is that the shared beliefs can severely constrain the *process* of strategy-making, resulting in the inappropriate process outcomes explained in Chapter 1 (i.e. "impoverished" or "blinkered" strategies).

The result of the actions of all the individuals determines the emerging strategy of the organization. We can argue that organizational processes influence the way individuals see the world, their values and beliefs, but that these influences operate along with the wider experiences of the individual listed above. The way individuals see the world affects the way they behave (the decisions they make, the actions they take). Collectively, these actions result in the organization's "realized strategy". Thus, the way we see the world affects the way we behave, and the collective behaviours of all the individuals in the organization decide the "way things get done around here".

Although this is a necessarily simplified representation of much more complex processes, this model will enable us to explore some important issues in the strategy–culture area. First, we shall set out the more important organizational processes within the organization, adding to the brief summary of processes introduced in Chapter 5.

Organizational processes

Organizational processes influence, and to some extent are, the culture of the organization. These processes can be divided into six categories: *grouping; power; controls and rewards; management styles; routines;* and *stories and symbols.* The categories are not totally distinct, and there are strong interrelationships between them. However, to assist our understanding of culture we shall consider each category in turn.

Organizational processes can be deliberate or emergent. Deliberate processes are those that are intended by top management; emergent processes evolve organically within the organization and may or may not be supportive of top management intentions.

Grouping

The way the organization specializes is a key dimension of culture. As was suggested in the previous chapter, functional specialization can encourage parochial attitudes and values that may impede cooperation across the organization. Typically unhelpful outcomes of parochialism are: "not invented here", therefore it can't be any good; and, "it's not our fault/problem", it must be that of marketing/engineering/ operations. More subtle manifestations of the problem are differences in beliefs that can emerge if individuals only have experience of working in one function. Hence someone with sales experience is likely to spot the firm's lack of competitiveness earlier than most: they may well see, for instance, that the reason for the poor performance is the limited product range. Another manager with operations experience may come to a quite different view, seeing the problem as one of high production costs compounded by an unnecessary proliferation of product variants.

In some organizations the position of chief executive officer has tended to be occupied by a representative of the same function over the years: for example, the chief executive is always an accountant, or the top jobs always go to engineers. This can be partly explained by the tendency of people to appoint those that they are most comfortable with. Thus an engineer in the top position may well feel most at ease with like-minded managers, those with whom he has many points of contact through shared or similar past experiences. The problem here for strategy-making is that a very similar way of viewing the world is perpetuated at the very top of the organization. This can seriously impede the decision-making processes, reducing the quality of debate and the challenge to received and shared wisdom.

The bases of specialization that we explored in Chapter 5 play a crucial role in signalling to members of the organization what is important. A strong functional specialization therefore indicates that the development of particular skills and expertise is crucial. Conversely, if staff are grouped according to customer types, markets, projects or products, different priorities are being signalled.

Informal groupings evolve spontaneously, a process that is facilitated by people being located together. Even though the formal structure may not require certain staff to interact, if they are located together, informal groups will emerge. For example, managers may prefer to interact informally with their peers, rather than their subordinates. It is through interactions with others that opinions can be formed. If these interactions are formally managed – that is, in a planned meeting or presentation – then the process of attitude formation may to some extent be under the control of top management. However, attitudes formed through informal interactions may run counter to the management's desired outcomes. Informal opinion leaders can powerfully affect the way certain management actions and pronouncements are received.

Informal networks can be a critical aspect of the way the organization works. Ericsson, the Swedish based multinational, allows the CEOs of its hundreds of subsidiaries a great deal of autonomy; they are able to commit large capital sums to projects without the involvement of senior staff at headquarters. But these CEOs have grown up within the Ericsson culture, and they understand that with the authority to commit large sums of the corporation's capital there is a strong obligation to behave responsibly. They also make extensive use of an informal network that spans the globe, using contacts to help with problems and passing on leads to more appropriately placed colleagues. The difficulty that Ericsson now faces is that they are acquiring many new businesses, and the traditional way of managing subsidiaries, which relies on the appointed CEOs being imbued with the Ericsson culture, no longer works where the acquired firm retains the original management.

Power

The power to make decisions or to block the implementation of decisions is an important dimension in the strategy–culture relationship. In some organizations, decision-making is very decentralized, and staff at lower levels are allowed to make quite important operational decisions. In other organizations, the power to decide even quite trivial matters is centralized at the apex of the structure. This extreme form of centralization can emerge when, for example, the organization is in crisis; more routinely, it can result from strong pressure on the chief executive from corporate headquarters.

Where decision-making is seen to be excessively centralized it is likely that the management at lower levels will either be frustrated, and the more able will leave, or they may develop behaviours that are passive and dependent, and no initiative is exercised. Attempts to change this, to "empower" managers, may well founder if the managers feel threatened. Their past experiences may not have given them the confidence to make more critical decisions.

Formal power or authority is vested in management positions in the structure. In recent years there have been attempts to reduce the number of hierarchical levels through delayering, both to reduce costs and, more symbolically, to improve relationships and communication between the top and the bottom of the structure. Often delayering can result in "empowerment" by default: if there is no manager available any more to ask, then we have to make the decision ourselves.

Informal power is power that individuals or groups may have which lies outside the formal hierarchy. Informal power can derive from the following two main sources:

1. *Dependence* High dependence of the organization on the individual or group. This is a particular issue in professional organizations (e.g. a hospital's dependence on consultants), but it may also emerge when particular groups have the ability to significantly affect the organization's activity, for example a high dependence on sales staff, or maintenance or computer operations

2. *Control of information* Information is power, and provision or withholding of information can give individuals influence.

Controls and rewards

"What gets measured, gets done": the control systems of the organization signal priorities. Typically, control systems are based on activities and outputs that lend themselves to quantitative measurement: cost, budgets, sales targets, capacity utilization, overheads and so on. This can lead to a distortion of effort towards those activities that are measured, which may not be in line with the intended strategy. For example, if the intended strategy stresses customer service priorities, but the control systems continue to emphasize cost containment, then the realized strategy may well reflect the control systems rather than the intended strategy.

Similarly, people take notice of which behaviours are rewarded. The desire to be recognized and to be given approval through rewards, which need not be purely monetary – status, praise and public recognition may all be powerful motivators – appears to be a core need in individuals. Behaviours that are rewarded are likely to be imitated: as with the control systems, therefore, rewards should reinforce the intended strategy.

Management styles

Management or leadership style has been a focus of interest for many years. Management style has been variously categorized, but most approaches recognize differences between autocratic and participative or consultative styles. Attempts have been made to identify more effective management styles, culminating in a contingency approach that suggests that there is no one best way to manage – it all depends on the situation.

Running alongside the more formal, academic exploration of the effects of style, there has been a stream of more populist management literature, including the "great man" and "excellence" books based on acknowledged success stories. An important difference between these approaches and the contingency theories is that the great man and excellence schools advocate that managers adopt "excellence" behaviours regardless of their situation. According to these writers, there is one *best* way to manage, which usually involves managers listening to staff, empowering them, and then setting out broad, inspiring "visions" to guide their decisions.

In contrast, the contingency approach suggests that certain types of organization encourage or even require management styles that are quite different: for example, the machine organization is highly centralized, with an autocratic management obsessed with control and discipline; an organic adhocracy, on the other hand, may require a consultative and informal management style.

As argued earlier, the organizational processes identified are not watertight compartments. For example, management style is influenced by the formal power structure, and the extent and degree of specialization. Writers such as Mintzberg and Miller use the terms "configuration" and "gestalt" to refer to particular combinations of structure and processes that seem to fit together – the machine organization would be one configuration. The organizational structures and processes are mutually reinforcing. If this is the case, then it may be extremely difficult to try to change one process dimension without concurrently trying to change other dimensions in order to create a new, mutually reinforcing set of structures and processes – a move from one configuration to another.

To cite a common instance of this problem: it may be questioned whether a technique such as "quality circles" can be successfully introduced into a machine organization that is autocratic, centralized and obsessed with control. For quality circles to work, shop floor employees must be trusted by management, and credited with the ability to analyze quality problems and recommend solutions. If the prevailing beliefs and attitudes of management are that employees cannot be trusted, cannot exercise initiative, and must be continually supervised and controlled, then quality circles will never work.

The prevailing style of management in a firm is clearly an important aspect of its culture. The behaviour of individual senior managers plays a crucial role in signalling to staff what is important, and what is appropriate behaviour. Subordinates watch their bosses very carefully. If they detect differences between the espoused strategy (e.g. the customer is number one) and top management behaviour (e.g. the chief executive is number one!), it is the latter behaviour that is most likely to shape opinions. The actions of the chief executive assume symbolic importance. The way chief executives use their time signals their priorities. This time could be spent meeting important customers, holding senior management meetings, attending committees at corporate HQ, addressing each and every customer relations training course, or walking around the factory discussing quality problems with shop floor workers. The choices chief executives make in allocating their time can have a profound influence in shaping the attitudes and values of subordinates. If chief executives bother to learn the names of every member of the organization this clearly signals to even the most junior staff that they are a valued part of the organization: for example, the headmaster who knows the name of all 2,000 children in the school.

Routines

Routines are essentially the way work gets done in the organization. They can be tightly specified procedures, deliberately established to deal with predictable activities (e.g. ordering components, evaluating a capital expenditure proposal). They can also be highly emergent in nature, taking the form of generally accepted and understood ways of working that have never been explicitly agreed or even discussed: for example, new product ideas always start in the research department.

Because routines are so embedded in the organization, they can prove to be major obstacles to change. Formalized routines and procedures at least have the merit of being explicit, so they can be challenged and replaced. It is implicit routines that can exercise an insidious and profound influence on behaviour. Because they are implied, accepted and understood they can be ways of working which are so obvious that individuals in the organization could not conceive of other ways in which things could be done. As a result, these informal routines can be extremely difficult to identify, let alone change, and it requires a great deal of challenging reflection to uncover such embedded behaviours.

The importance of the part played by routines in any organization cannot be overstated: routines are the very fabric of an organization. Without them, people would have to re-create the organization every day. Routines provide an essential rhythm and stability to day-to-day activity. However, the downside is that, if the intended strategy requires a shift in the way the organization is behaving, the taken-for-granted routines must be changed. It is at this very mundane but fundamental level of activity that many of the problems of strategic change lie.

In Chapter 3 we highlighted the importance of organizational know-how in delivering advantage. This shared expertise clearly has a cultural dimension. Know-how is embedded in the routine ways things are done in the organization. Therefore, although some routines may be inefficient and be holding the firm back, others may be the very essence of advantage. This poses a serious problem when attempts are made to change the organization. Some change programmes may inadvertently destroy know-how (e.g. delayering, or business process re-engineering).

To avoid this outcome the management need to develop a sophisticated insight into the unique sources of advantage in the firm, and to ensure that these sources are nurtured, not destroyed. The means–end (or "cause–effect") analysis introduced in Chapter 3 can be helpful in uncovering the strategic detail.

A particular cultural form of routine is the "ritual". Illustration 6.2 groups organizational rituals into nine categories or types, with some examples of each type. Rituals serve as cultural processes that can operate to facilitate or obstruct change in the organization. They help to provide some of the "glue" that bonds people to the organization.

Stories and symbols

Stories recounted by members of the organization play a central role in preserving and perpetuating the culture. They help to link the present with the past, they act to bind people together, when, for example, people gather in the bar to recount past successes or failures, and they can operate as a kind of cultural shorthand to communicate quite complex values and beliefs. Thus stories of heroes and villains help to signal appropriate behaviours. In contrast, stories about mavericks who buck the system help us to understand what the unstated norms of the organization are.

Symbols are organizational activities or artefacts that convey meaning. We are familiar with symbols of status: cars, desk size, personal assistants, and dining facilities, but more subtle symbols can play an important part in preserving shared values and beliefs. For example, the location of a corporate headquarters can help to convey the values of the business: is it in the heart of the City of London, or next door to one of the manufacturing sites? Corporate logos and the changing of them have assumed a level of importance recently, largely due to an awareness that they signify what the organization stands for – changing the logo signifies a break with the past. Language also acts symbolically: if customers are referred to as "punters" or "bums on seats" this conveys a certain set of attitudes – contrast this language with "guests" or "delegates". Actions can have a powerful symbolic influence: for instance the chief executive takes a pay cut, a "director of quality" is appointed, a shop steward is sacked.

6.2 **Some examples of rituals**

Ritual type	Subcategories
Challenge	New appointments/transfers Introduction of new ideas Old way goes Publication of the need to change Widespread redundancy New structures Project teams
Resistance	Covert grumblings Overt counter-actions Questions/doubts Sticking to the old ways
Conflict reduction	Actions taken Forums/committees set up Notes provided
Degradation	Closure of site/division Job loss Removal of old order Rationalization Transfers
Enhancement	Awards Conditions of employment Promotion Power related Publications Verbal acknowledgements
Integration	Written communications Structure changes Organization-wide briefings Social events Team-based briefings Corporate identify
Passage/organizational passage	Announcements/launches Building related Person related Recruitment Structure Training

Ritual type	Subcategories
Renewal	Appointments/transfers
	Consultants
	Specific focus/emphasis
	Reviews
	Schemes/projects
	Training
	Working parties/teams
Sense-making	Speculation/discussion
	Rumours

(Source: S. Martin, J. Newton and G. Johnson, "The use of rituals within organizational change processes", paper presented at the BAM Conference, Sheffield, 1995.)

Some firms use stage-managed events to signal change or enthuse staff. Motivational sales conferences are highly symbolic events. The prestigious venue, the celebrity speaker, and the use of music, video images and staging for dramatic effect, combine to elevate the conference into a cultural event.

These and other organizational processes, both deliberate and emergent in nature, influence the way members of the organization see the world. We shall now look at these cognitive processes in a little more detail.

Cognitive processes

Here we are referring to the beliefs, assumptions, attitudes and values held by individuals. These are formed by past experiences, which may or may not be strongly associated with the organization. For example, some firms have policies that encourage staff to stay with the firm for their entire careers. In these firms, we would expect the influence of the organization to loom very large in the cognitions of members. In a newly established firm, however, or in one in which there has been considerable staff turnover, members will not have undergone the same experiences and are therefore less likely to hold the same set of beliefs and values. The range of past experiences is likely to be great in these organizations, and consequently the ability of organizational processes to inculcate a shared set of values and beliefs is reduced.

Some organizations address this problem explicitly with extensive periods of training and indoctrination (e.g. the army, and some large multinationals). These indoctrination processes are obviously more effective if the new members have reasonably congruent beliefs and values to start with, so selection becomes critical. If this is not possible – if, for instance, the army has conscription – then elaborate processes, like "basic training" in the army, are used to strip out the values and beliefs new entrants come in with, so that the required values can be introduced. The advantage of recruiting school and college leavers into the organization is that it is easier to inculcate required values and beliefs into a person if someone else has not reached them first: there is more of a "clean sheet" to fill in. This is one of the reasons that Nissan set up its UK production plant far away from the traditional car-making centres like Birmingham. Emergent processes can, however, undermine deliberate attempts to shape beliefs and values. The hard work of the training and induction staff can be rapidly undermined by the influence of a cynical informal leader.

Shared beliefs and values can be a source of competitive advantage, as long as they are in line with an appropriate strategy. However, if the firms in an industry are staffed largely by people with little experience of working in any other industry, then a shared set of beliefs and assumptions is likely to emerge across the industry. There can be problems with such an industry "recipe", where there are shared beliefs about how to compete, what the customers value, and so on, and there may be advantages to be gained by a firm successfully challenging the accepted rules of the game. (Illustration 6.3 sets out the industry "recipe" for Scottish knitwear manufacturers.) In order to mount such a challenge the management of a firm already inside the industry has to free itself from those unstated, implicit beliefs, which, by definition, is something that is not easily done. Therefore it is often an outsider who successfully challenges these widely held assumptions in an industry. The outsider either comes in to take control of an incumbent firm or is a new entrant – but, as we saw in Chapter 1, often the successful new entrant simply applies a recipe that brought success in another industry.

Recipes operate at the level of the organization as well. Gerry Johnson in "Rethinking Incrementalism" (*Strategic Management Journal*, vol. 9, 1 (1988)) has called the organization's recipe the "paradigm". The paradigm consists of the beliefs and assumptions that are held in

6.3 The Scottish knitwear manufacturers' "industry recipe"

Insularity and oligopolistic competition amongst the Scottish knitwear manufacturers limits their vision of the marketplace.

The manufacturers in the Scottish knitwear industry have a set of beliefs and assumptions which are commonly held and taken for granted. These concern the nature of the industry and success strategies. The following beliefs and assumptions are the "industry recipe":

- ◆ The Scottish manufacturers produce top-quality cashmere pullovers.

- ◆ The Scottish manufacturers' customers are "individuals in the top 2–5 per cent of income groups".

- ◆ No other producers can manufacture the kind of sweaters that they produce.

- ◆ Competition only comes from among themselves.

- ◆ They don't consider textile manufacturers from outside the region as a threat.

- ◆ They believe that "high fashion is not the business of Scottish firms", preferring traditional designs of "classical elegance".

- ◆ They disapprove of severe price competition.

- ◆ They believe that "Scottish spinners are the finest in the world".

This industry recipe has formed due to similar schooling, family backgrounds, career paths, proximity of location (both private and work), and national culture.

The effect of the assumptions and beliefs is to influence the ability of these industrialists to formulate and implement effective strategies. For them, the recipe is the key to success and it is taken for granted – it blinkers them and they don't challenge it. All the Scottish manufacturers have similar strategies: they mainly compete with each other on design and their strategies are conservative and only slowly evolve with changes in the marketplace. So, strategy formulation arises mainly from the managers' own cognitive processes. Moreover, because the firms gather information through their mature distribution networks, a self-fulfilling prophecy is created in which they only survey their existing customers. Therefore, they don't recognize the need for market research, for unbiased market information or for competitor analysis. Their strategic choices are limited by the industry recipe.

(Source: Adapted by V. Ambrosini from J. F. Porac, H. Thomas and C. Baden-Fuller, "Competitive groups as cognitive communities: the case of Scottish knitwear manufacturers", *Journal of Management Studies*, vol. 26 (1989), pp. 397–416.)

common and taken for granted in the organization. As we have seen above, the influence of organizational processes on individual cognitions is greatest when members have shared the same past experiences. Strong paradigms are likely to exist, then, in firms that recruit school and college leavers, who stay in the firm for most of their careers, and where policies support internal promotions. The shared past experiences are likely to lead to shared world views.

Strong paradigms can make it extremely difficult for organizations to change strategic direction. Even when the members of the top management try to construct strategies based on analysis and hard facts, their interpretation of the analysis is coloured by their shared beliefs and assumptions. They will tend to place emphasis on "facts" that support their world view, and to discount or even ignore results that challenge these firmly held assumptions. The real problem, however, is the "taken for grantedness" of these beliefs and assumptions. They operate on individual cognitions in a similar way to that in which routines operate at the level of the organization. They guide thought and shape interpretations of events: they are so understood that they are never discussed. If they are not brought to the surface in some way, they can never be openly challenged.

Behaviour

Behaviour is what people in the organization actually do, including the actions they take and the decisions they make. We have already explained the routine nature of most organizational activity. Behaviour that is routinized – either deliberately, or through custom and practice – is very difficult to change.

Routines that are deeply embedded can be a source of great stability in times of turmoil and uncertainty. For example, a building society underwent a succession of major strategic shifts over a period of three years: takeover by a rival society, branch closures and rationalization, the introduction of more banking services, and the stripping out of two layers of management. During this period, the staff at branch level were confused and demoralized, so they relied on embedded routine behaviours to provide some much needed stability and security during this time of turbulence. One senior manager observed that the branches, falling back on tried and accepted ways of behaving, actually kept the society functioning, and if they had not behaved in that way the society may well not have survived. Though embedded routines can provide stability, however, problems emerge when these routines hold back the organization. Their very embeddedness can act as a serious barrier to change.

People's behaviour is obviously influenced by their perceptions of what is important. What they perceive to be the priorities in the organization will be influenced by the internal and external processes we have been exploring in this chapter. In some professional organizations (e.g. law firms, hospitals), individual professionals may well be strongly influenced by external, non-organizational sources. They owe their allegiance to their profession first and the organization second. Hence, in certain circumstances, their behaviour may not be in line with the intentions of senior management.

If a high degree of value congruence is achieved in the organization, staff can be expected to behave in appropriate ways without the need for formal control and supervision. These organizations are capable of operating in predictable ways even when the staff are geographically dispersed. If the recruiting processes help to select people whose values are already in line with those of the organization, so much the better.

At one extreme, there may be organizations whose members all have values and beliefs that are very similar; at the other extreme, the organization may bring together people with quite diverse beliefs and values that have been born out of their different experiences. Diversity of beliefs and values can be helpful: decisions should be informed by a wide range of views and experience, and the organization should be capable of adapting and changing its activity.

Realized strategy and performance

The collective behaviour of the members of the organization that emerges from the processes and influences outlined above determines the *realized* strategy, which may or may not be in line with the *intended* strategy. Intended strategies are implemented through the organizational processes discussed in this chapter. If there is a failure in implementation, the organizational processes have failed to affect behaviour in the desired ways. These issues are explored further in the next chapter.

Should there be no clear intended strategy, the realized strategy will emerge in an unplanned, incremental fashion. This may lead to acceptable performance – the organization tends to adjust in an organic way to changes in its environment. However, cultural processes can impede the process of adjustment and adaptation to a changing environment, and this is likely to lead to poor performance. Routines embedded in the organization that were appropriate in the past are now significant barriers to change – systems, styles and structures preserve the status quo. Often, the decline in performance that results from an increasing lack of alignment between the organization and its environment acts as a trigger for change, forcing the top management to explicitly address the strategy and to set in motion a change process within the organization.

Illustration 6.4 describes TVR, a small sports car manufacturer based in Blackpool, in the north-west of England. This company has been successfully competing in the sports-car market against industry giants like Porsche. It would seem that TVR's ability to succeed stems from the particular "way things are done" in the organization. A strong sense of a TVR culture emerges from the illustration. There are references to management style, stories, and core values, and a "genial modesty" which pervades the organization. Clearly, this culture can be a source of sustained advantage because it is difficult to replicate elsewhere. But it is vulnerable. If a new CEO was appointed who did not appreciate the subtle but critical role TVR's culture plays in its success, there is a danger that it could be destroyed.

So what?

Some of the practical implications of the arguments set out in this chapter are as follows:

♦ Culture is critical. As we saw in Chapter 3, sources of advantage are increasingly being identified with more complex and subtle phenomena like tacit knowledge, embedded routines and shared values. We therefore need to develop some understanding of our organization's culture to avoid, at the minimum, inadvertently destroying a source of advantage.

6.4 **Racing cert – from Blackpool**

The Morris Minor parked outside a motley row of industrial buildings in the back end of Blackpool is in a space labelled "racing". The mismatch cheerfully suits TVR Engineering. Irreverent laughter is silenced by recent achievements. The high-performance minnow, based across the road from a rubbish dump, stunned the Motor Show recently by unveiling two new engines which a team of 50 engineers will manufacture at its Coventry plant. "It's easier for us because we are designing them to be built by hand, which means that a trained engine builder can do much more complicated manoeuvres than any robot can," said one engineer. "The tooling costs are much lower for us and we are also designing them for power and strength and a bit of a lumpy tick-over which would be a disaster for Rolls-Royce."

The company shies away from comparisons with mass market car-makers, who may not have the same ratio of engineers willing to work until 1 a.m. The staff admit to having "TVR written through us like a stick of rock". "The internal joke is that we didn't have a budget for developing engines, but we exceeded it by a factor of four," says one employee.

Direct comparisons with the world's biggest car-makers are misleading. But when Ford announced it was developing a new diesel engine at Dagenham last year it said it needed to invest £200m. in development and tooling alone.

Next March the Blackpool motor industry will begin its first big assault on international GTI motor racing in Italy, with Ferrari and Porsche among the intended victims. It will mark a pit-stop debut for the new 660 hp engine in a high-performance car which is also meant for the road. The car, known as Project 12/7, is the gleaming silver monster parked in a workshop labelled GTI. "This is the real toyshop," says an employee. The company went abroad in the 1960s, competing at Le Mans and in the Tulip Rally, "but this is the first time we have had a pukka international GT team," said a spokesman. "In terms of turnover, more of our resources go to racing than any other car manufacturer."

Blackpool, the rumbustuous Lancashire seaside resort, has kept quiet about its engineering pedigree. Jaguar began its rise there, producing Swallow motorcycle sidecars. TVR made its first sports cars in 1949, two years after engineer Trevor Wilkinson developed his own car using an Alvis Firebird chassis. The company changed hands frequently for a decade, but since the 1960s there have been only two owners.

TVR emphasizes its northern credentials. A new model unveiling at the Motor Show two years ago was graced with the actress from the

Boddington's advertisements and celebrated with the Manchester-brewed bitter instead of champagne. The company can afford to act as motor industry court jester. When it exhibited the Griffith at the 1990 Birmingham Motor Show, orders were placed every eight minutes. Today, the company with the 5 mph speed restriction outside and the 160 mph-plus sports cars inside is producing around thirty-five cars a week. Record sales in 1995 have risen a further 50 per cent this year and the workforce has edged over 600.

Japan takes the lion's share of the 20 per cent of output that is exported, with personal orders going "all over the place from Puerto Rico to Poland".

Chimaera, Cerbera and Griffith 500 are the main models, selling at between £30,650 and £39,800. Those with a yearning for optional extras could spend another £6,445. Each car takes more than four weeks to build and each is built to order from its own specification sheet, which can include alterations for the driver's physique. Waiting lists are up to a year long.

Vehicles retain their values. One 1991 model, originally sold for £23,000 and no longer in production, was recently sold for £22,500. Despite such stories the company boasts a "classless" clientele, united by their enthusiasm for driving. The price tags are modest compared with rivals, the company claims, contrasting its Cerbera with a Porsche costing £25,000 more. Its drive into international motor racing is linked to giving TVR more recognition. "We are going out there and writing our own history," said company spokesman Ben Samuelson. "People are looking at Peter Wheeler (the owner-chairman) in the way they used to look at Colin Chapman." TVR takes a pride in being unorthodox. The company has doubled the size of its site in the last year, but space remains at a premium and white body shells are stored on flat roofs. Cars are assembled in open-plan offices. "I can't imagine working anywhere else, where there's no politics," said one executive.

Damien McTaggart and Nick Coughlan, the stylists, move quickly from sketching ideas into sculpting them in polyurethane foam. Potential designs are shown at motor shows, to test public reaction. Production also begins with sculptures; the shape of the body moulds into which layers of glass fibre are pressed by hand. Steel chassis are constructed on individual frames. After sanding, the bodies are primed and up to thirty-five coats of paint applied. The company offers 10,000 shades. One woman sent her ski boots for a match. The company assembles its own wiring and builds its own seats, even putting together the black boxes for the cars' electronics. Such flexibility is seen as essential in the production of "bespoke" models, and allows short runs and changes. "We don't make plans," said one executive.

"There's no committee that sits down and says: 'Right, the five year plan is this.' "

Rather, expansion will be limited by a site already approaching capacity in a company which has just taken delivery of its first car transporters capable of handling more than three cars.

Genial modesty will also continue. "It would be most unlike TVR to suggest there are lessons for the rest of the motor industry, for us to say: 'This is the way we do it and this is the right way'; that would be total anathema. The philosophy of the company is not to have a philosophy." This type of thinking baffled a high-ranking executive from Mercedes. He was intrigued by a story of how a design model was altered by the chairman's dog. Company legend says the dog was lunging at an engineer, but missed and took a lump out of a design prototype. The model has proved highly effective. The executive was inquisitive. "So where", he asked, "do we get these dogs?"

(Source: *Guardian*, Saturday, 30 November 1996.)

More importantly, if we can understand some of the complexity involved here, we are more able to nurture what is good about the culture, challenge and change what may be barriers, and replicate and promulgate cultural ''best practice'' as the organization expands.

◆ We need to surface and challenge our underlying assumptions and beliefs. What assumptions do we make, for example, about what we think we are good at? Who we think we compete with? What we think causes success around here? What we think customers value in our products?

◆ If we acquire another business we need to be alert to the subtle cultural differences between us and the acquired firm.

Summary

In this chapter we have examined the links between strategy and culture. Culture is increasingly of interest to strategists because it influences both the formulation and the implementation of strategy. Using a simple model, we initially disaggregated cultural processes into distinct categories. Organization processes included: grouping, informal and formal power relationships, control and reward systems, management style, stories and symbols. We highlighted the importance of routines in preserving stability and we linked the concept of routines back to our arguments concerning know-how as a source of inimitable advantage advanced in Chapter 3. The category *cognitive processes* captured important contributions to our understanding of strategy processes, particularly the notions of industry recipe and organizational paradigms.

CHAPTER 7

Managing strategic change

We argued in the previous chapter that culture plays a central role in the strategy process. Therefore, in order to understand some of the issues in managing strategic change it is appropriate to use the cultural perspective developed in the last chapter (see Figure 6.1).

Culture and strategic change

In many mainstream strategy textbooks, strategy implementation is treated as a sequential step following on from strategy formulation. Those who have wrestled with the problems of managing strategic change, however, can find it difficult to identify with an orderly and rational formulation/implementation sequence. Managing strategic change is often messy, complex and stressful. Routines – the old ways of doing things – often exert a powerful influence. And even though there may be intellectual agreement and understanding of the need for change, routine ways of behaving can predominate. This is probably because the routines are embedded in an organizational structure that supports behaviour in line with the routines, and makes behaviour outside the routines quite difficult. For example, the functional structure, the power relationships, the way people relate and interact, and the control systems are congruent with the old routines, not the new intended strategy.

Frequently, there is overwhelming pressure to retain existing ways of behaving, and to change behaviour in these circumstances will therefore probably require more than merely an intellectual agreement to change. The structures and processes in which the old routines are embedded must be changed as well. This would suggest that real strategic change can only be achieved through changes in cultural processes and that such changes will have to be tackled on a broad front in which the many interlocking dimensions of culture – structures, systems, symbols and so on – are addressed.

A further implication of this line of reasoning is that if implementation is attempted through existing structures and processes it is possible that the culture will *absorb, dilute and dissipate* the intended strategy. Moreover, if the influence of the culture in preserving old routines is pervasive, it is absolutely vital that the management team trying to effect change not only understand and agree with the strategy, but are also highly committed to it themselves and firmly believe that change is essential.

As we explored in Chapter 1, there may be a relationship between the quality of the content of a strategy (i.e. what the strategy is about), and the quality of commitment to change the organization in line with the intended strategy. It may well be desirable to trade off the content quality of the strategy in order to improve the level of commitment to change.

Commitment is usually generated through *involvement*. If the members of the executive team feel that the strategy is really theirs, that they own the strategy, then the required changes, even though they may be painful and difficult, are much more likely to be driven through. So it is vital that the process of strategy-making is one that generates commitment to change: this suggests that the strategy must be decided by those executives who will be responsible for its implementation. However, we noted in the last chapter that the members of a management team may be constrained by a paradigm. They may hold a set of beliefs and assumptions about, for example, their strengths, customer needs and competitors' capabilities that are implicit and never discussed. If strategy-making is left entirely to this group, there is a danger that the quality of debate and the challenging of assumptions that are required to produce high-quality strategic thinking will not take place. The resulting strategy is most likely to be some incremental adjustment to existing patterns of activity. Even if analytical processes are used, there is a danger that the results of analysis will be used *selectively* to justify the strategy that has emerged from past ad hoc, incremental decisions.

So we have a dilemma. If the strategy is left to "objective outsiders" – for example, the staff in the strategic planning department, or external consultants – the quality of the strategy may be high but the chances of it being implemented may be low. However, if the members of the executive team construct the strategy, there is a danger that they may generate a large degree of commitment to the "wrong" strategy. What is required are processes that mitigate the dangers of paradigm-dominated thinking, but that capitalize on the benefits of involvement. Such processes should lead to high levels of commitment towards a sound strategic direction.

Content quality versus process quality

Increasingly, strategy consultants are seeking to establish longer-term relationships with their clients. In the past the task of the strategy consultant was to come in as objective outsider, conduct an extensive analysis of the firm's strategic situation, and make strategy recommendations. At this point, the report would be handed over to the firm's management and the consultants would leave the scene.

Now, more and more consultants are working *with* their clients, helping them to think through the strategic situation they are facing, and facilitating the process of strategy formulation and implementation. The emphasis has shifted away from the content of the strategy towards improving the quality of the strategy process. By helping the members of the top management team in their strategy deliberations, the consultants can generate the necessary commitment to the emerging strategy, but at the same time they can act as devil's advocates, challenging and evaluating the assumptions held by the team. They are also able to provide more objective data on which to base decisions.

The techniques and frameworks that have been set out in this book can be used to expose the taken-for-granted assumptions of the team, and, in so doing, the influence of the paradigm in shaping perceptions and understanding can be reduced.

Triggering change

We can refer to our culture model set out in Chapter 6 to explore some issues in the change process. In Figure 7.1 we have reproduced the model.

Relationship 1 between the external environment and the organization is most keenly felt by "boundary spanning" staff like sales people.

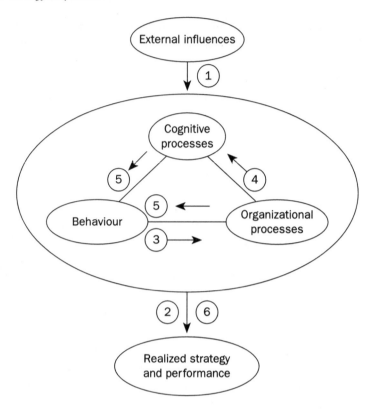

Figure 7.1 *Culture and change relationships*

Often, early signals of the need for change are picked up by these staff. They sense that the existing products and services are becoming uncompetitive, or they start to encounter a new player in the market. However, often these signals fail to reach top managers early enough, or even if they do, the messages contained within them lose some of their impact as they are reinterpreted to justify the current ways of doing things.

It is often only when a crisis is precipitated, usually in the form of a serious deterioration in performance (Relationship 2), that senior executives grasp the nettle of change. However, this may be too late to save the firm. The usual action that flows from this realization is cost-cutting in all its various forms: the crisis leads to staff lay-offs, delayering, downsizing, drastic trimming of the softer budgets like training, research and development, and even to plant closures. These cuts are easy to understand and relatively straightforward to implement, although they can be painful for those adversely affected. At this stage in the change process, there is no sense of a new strategy or vision informing these actions. The management are merely destroying parts of the past (Relationship 3).

In order to embark upon a new phase of development, there needs to be some sense of a new future, a vision or strategy that builds rather than destroys the organization. Relationship 4 suggests that for this to happen there may need to be structural and process changes first. The most obvious is the arrival of a new CEO with ways of thinking new to the organization.

If a new strategy is to be realized it has to affect routine behaviours. Successful implementation of the new strategy would manifest itself through new routines being embedded in the organization (Relationship 5), leading to the emergence of the new realized strategy (Relationship 6). If it is the right strategy for the firm, it should lead to more sustained performance improvements than simply those stemming from cost-cutting.

In the rest of this chapter, we consider a range of process interventions that can help bring about significant change in the organization. I refer to the culture model to assess the role and contribution of each prescription.

The mission statement

We begin with mission statements, which seem to have a very mixed press. When working with executives two contrasting opinions appear about the usefulness of missions. Most executives view them rather cynically. However, a minority value them and perceive them to be hugely influential in their organizations. I rarely encounter executives with moderate views about mission statements. They either love them or hate them. Clearly, there must be some contextual or process factors that are causing these extreme reactions. We shall return to these following a brief summary of mission statements.

The role of the mission statement

Mission statements are supposed to capture the essence of the firm's strategy in a concise statement of intent. They may be very brief indeed, like "A Personal Computer in Every Home" or Komatsu's "Encircle Caterpillar", or they may extend to several paragraphs. Sometimes they take on a rather dry and objective tone that sets out broad guidelines for the organization; others are very visionary and inspirational.

However, like the fate of many management fads, the quality of the implementation of the idea can be very poor. Many organizations have mission statements, but few managers, even those in senior positions, could tell you what is in the statement. Those that can remember them may well not *believe* in the statements made. This is a pity, because a good mission statement can play a powerful part in strategic change. It can also *empower* managers at the apex of the organization, providing them with the confidence to make tough decisions that are in line with the agreed mission.

If the statement is to play this role, it needs to be carefully crafted, and we shall now set out some useful guidelines for drawing up a mission statement.

The mission statement: some guidelines

The purpose of the mission statement is to communicate to those *inside* the organization the broad ground rules that the organization has set itself in conducting its business, and it should therefore have the following characteristics:

- ◆ It should be a broadly framed and *enduring statement of intent*.

- ◆ It should be essentially an *internal working document*.

The statement should set out as clearly as possible the essence of the competitive strategy, as follows:

- ◆ the *target markets* (and segments);

- ◆ how competitive advantage will be gained in those markets;

- ◆ how competitive advantage will be translated into superior profitability (including cost management);

- ◆ a summary (if appropriate) of the required competences to achieve the competitive strategy;

- ◆ how success will be measured; and

◆   attitudes to growth, diversification and to financing.

It may also be appropriate to include statements of intent towards various stakeholders, staff, society, and the local community.

The statement needs to be concise, but at the same time it must provide unambiguous guidance. It is this last requirement that makes mission statements so difficult to get right. Although brevity is desirable, if it results in ambiguity or, worse still, a set of bland and generalized "motherhood" clichés, the statement will not be a living document. It will be viewed cynically and seen as irrelevant.

Although it may be desirable to include value statements about concern for employees or the environment, this should only be done if the team members believe in them sufficiently to back them up with visible actions. If the team puts in pious statements for public and/or employee relations purposes that it has no real intention of implementing, then as soon as one piece of evidence is found that demonstrates a lack of commitment to the espoused values, the mission statement as a whole will fall into disrepute.

As a working document for managers, the statement should be as tough and as clear as possible. If a statement is required for PR purposes, then one should be drawn up separately to meet this requirement. The trap of trying to construct one statement to satisfy two requirements should be avoided, since the usual result of the attempt is a bland "wish list" that satisfies neither need well.

In order to draw up a mission statement, the management team must engage in a full-scale strategic analysis. When setting the guidelines for the medium-term strategy of the firm, markets must be analyzed, trends in customers' needs understood, and the relative performance of competitors and the threat of entrants assessed. Choices must be made to move in to or out of particular markets or segments of markets. The competences required to deliver the strategy must be identified and target levels of attainment should be set: for example, the fastest new-product development cycle in the industry, or 99 per cent right first time.

In summarizing the essence of the competitive strategy it is sometimes useful to focus attention, first, on those product/service dimensions that are valued by customers and can be made *better than* those offered by the competitors, and, secondly, on those dimensions where the aim is to be *as good as* the competitors.

One way of judging how good the statement is, is to ask the following questions about it:

◆ Would a new manager entering the firm have a clear view, just from reading the mission statement, of what is trying to be achieved?

◆ Does each phrase and sentence help to clarify the firm's intentions? If one does not, why is it in there? Could it be taken out?

◆ Does the top team really believe in the statement (that means every word)? If not, it should be torn up and started again.

◆ Is it obvious how a whole set of schemes must be set in motion if the intentions in the statement are to be realized?

If there are substantial differences between the product markets that the firm intends to trade in, and if the capabilities required to gain advantage in these markets are also very different, it will probably be necessary to draw up more than one mission statement. If the firm prefers to have one overarching document at corporate level, this can be supplemented by a strategy statement for each substantial market or segment grouping.

As a rough guide, mission statements should have an effective life of at least two years. Bringing the organization into line with the intentions set out in the statement will take time, and people in the organization will need to see some stability in the direction the firm is taking if they are to commit themselves to the required changes. A continually changing mission statement will not be perceived as a credible document. Illustration 7.1 is a statement of values from Dun & Bradstreet. Whether this is a believable statement depends upon the extent to which these values are translatable into tangible action, and whether staff from the top downwards are clearly seen to act in line with these values. The statement of ethics can actually be operationalized. It suggests that the test would be whether staff have pride in the company. This can be tested through surveys and group discussions, benchmarks can be set, and progress or otherwise monitored. Thus even a seemingly vague and aspirational statement of values can be turned into something measurable. Similarly, customers' expectations could be measured

7.1 The Dun & Bradstreet Corporation statement of values

Illustration

As the men and women who are the Dun & Bradstreet Corporation, we are a team – *one company* united through shared values relating to our ethics, customers, ourselves and our shareowners.

Ethics
We will practise the highest standards of personal ethics and integrity, so that in all our relationships we can have pride in ourselves and our company.

Customers
We will strive relentlessly to exceed our customers' expectations, so that they will want to continue to do business with us.

Ourselves
We will respect and treat each other as individuals who want the opportunity to contribute and succeed. Each of us will be accountable for quality and continuous improvement in all we do. We will work to be the best.

Shareowners
We will accept our responsibility to be effective stewards of our shareowners' resources, so that through our performance shareowners are properly rewarded for their investment in Dun & Bradstreet.

By living and working in accordance with these values, everyone who is affected by our behaviour will say of us, "Customer focus is how they do business."

(Source: J. Humble, D. Jackson and A. Thomson, "The strategic power of corporate planning", *Long Range Planning*, vol. **27**.)

and monitored to check whether those expectations are indeed being exceeded. But there are still areas of some ambiguity in this statement: "We will work to be the best" – compared to whom? "Shareowners are properly rewarded" – what is a "proper" level of reward?

Looked at in this light, it is clear that the mission statement summarizes the output of an extensive process of strategic thinking. It should not, therefore, be drawn up at the *start* of such a process. If the mission statement captures the essence of the strategy, it can then be used as *the* key strategic document. A whole set of actions should then be driven by the mission statement.

The role of the mission statement in strategic change

Referring to Figure 7.1 we can assess the way in which a mission statement may assist in the process of cultural change. If the team that drafts the statement has not engaged in a challenging debate about strategy, the chances are that the statement will merely confirm past realized strategy. The cognitive processes of the group responsible for the mission may restrict and constrain the emerging vision to the extent that no real change is seen to be required to organization processes or behaviours. We should not underestimate the attractions of such an outcome. A mission that confirms, broadly, the legitimacy of the status quo also confirms the practices, routines and priorities of the past, and it justifies the existing structures and power relationships. A mission statement like this is likely to be warmly and actively supported by all those who benefit from the status quo.

Mission statements that call for significant shifts in the way things are done in the firm can come about in a variety of ways. They can be drawn up with the involvement of outside consultants, who, being in a more objective position, may be able to set out dispassionately the nature and the extent of the changes required. The chances of this statement impacting on the organization will depend upon the power relationships within the structure, particularly the extent to which the CEO backs the strategy set out by the consultants. Whether change is wholeheartedly adopted by other top-team members will depend on the degree to which they are dissatisfied personally with their current situations. A crisis precipitated by a serious deterioration in performance may persuade these executives that change is the only option. More positively, there may be attractions in pursuing the change of direction if the executive perceives positive outcomes for him- or herself.

For a top team to construct and be committed to a strategy of change themselves requires them to engage in new ways of thinking. While the impetus to explore new strategies may be encouraged by outside events – for example, performance problems, a new entrant into the market, or pressure from the corporate centre – the ability to conceive of new ways of doing things can certainly be facilitated by outsiders. These outsiders may be consultant facilitators who are able to inject new ways of analyzing and can import a wider base of experience; in other cases it may be a new CEO or other significant top-team member who injects new thinking. The CEO may have the advantage of past success, which both instils self-confidence and can inspire the rest of the team to take on the personal risks of changing.

I have had some involvement as a facilitator with top teams who are genuinely searching for a clearer sense of strategic direction. Where these teams come to some agreement about the broad thrust of their firm's strategy, and where they have been able to summarize this into a concise statement of strategic intent, the teams appear to be *empowered*. The clarification of the firm's strategy gives them confidence in making day-to-day operational decisions that may previously have been made on a more ad hoc basis. Thus, when confronted by a reporting manager requesting more staff or capital expenditure, the executive can refer to the strategy in making this judgement. If the manager's request is in line with the intended direction, then the request wins the executive's full support; if it does not support the strategy, the request is denied. This feeds down through the structure, empowering managers at lower levels. There is a sense of direction; middle managers might not agree with all of it, but at least there is a consistent ''line'' coming down from the top.

From mission statement into action

If the mission statement is to be a live document it must be translated into action. There is no obvious and foolproof way of doing this, but perhaps the least useful approach is to pass on the statement to the executives of each of the existing functions and have them interpret what it means to them. The main reason why this is unlikely to result in the required actions is that, if the statement does not merely endorse the strategy of the past, it will include statements of intent that will require changes to the current ways of doing things. If the statement is passed on to the existing functional heads, it is likely to be interpreted and absorbed into current functional routines. Referring to Figure 7.1, the intended strategy as an organizational process should initiate changes in cognitions that would lead, in turn, to changes in behaviour, but the intentions can be *reinterpreted* and comfortably absorbed into existing routines.

Using the status quo to change the status quo

The existing structures and processes in the organization support the current ways of doing things. Should the new strategy indicate that the organization needs to behave in different ways, a problem is likely to arise if the existing structures are the primary vehicle for implementing the changes. Current structures and processes may well distort and dilute the intended strategy to the point where no discernible change takes place.

If the intended strategy is implemented through the existing functional structure of the firm, it will be interpreted by functional managers in terms that make sense to them and in ways that reflect the types of activity which the function has previously been responsible for. However, it may be that critical actions are required that fall outside the traditional functional division of tasks. By translating the strategy only into behaviours that reflect the past functional specialization, actions that lie outside the existing functions, or, more typically, actions that cut across several existing functions, will not be picked up.

It may therefore be necessary to employ other structures and processes if significant changes to routine behaviour are required. Using structures and processes that lie outside the status quo should reduce the possibility that the intended strategy will become assimilated into existing routines.

Change processes

There are a number of ways in which organizations use processes outside the existing structures to effect strategic change. Four popular approaches are: *competence champions*; *project management*; *cross-functional teams*; and *reorganizing the structure*.

Competence champions

Here, the actions that are required to move the organization towards the intended strategy are grouped into broad required capabilities or competences. Examples of required or key competences might be:

◆ To attract and retain well-motivated, well-qualified staff.

- To achieve rapid new product introductions.

- To maximize the profitable business opportunities available in the after-market.

None of these required competences is particularly startling, but the problem lies in the fact that the existing functions are not delivering these capabilities. It is the role of the competence champion to drive forward the agreed sets of actions that are required to achieve each competence, and to be held accountable by the chief executive and the top team for progress towards improving this competence. The actions usually involve staff from several different functions working together in small teams, which means that if the competence champions are to influence staff from other departments, they must have power. This can be achieved in either of the following ways:

1. The competence champions are selected or volunteer from the group of top managers, bringing with them the formal and informal authority of their functional positions.

2. The champions are selected from a pool of high-flying middle/senior managers. They therefore have their own skills and abilities to influence people who may be senior to them, but they are also visibly empowered by the chief executive officer to whom they have a direct reporting line.

Project management

Project management is a well-established discipline that has evolved from the problems of managing large-scale, one-off projects such as dam building or sending a man to the moon. It requires the clear separation of the client role from that of project manager. The client sets the objectives of the project and is the ultimate judge of its success; the client can also terminate the project at any time. Usually, the project manager is assigned a multidisciplinary team to carry out the project, and the composition of the team may change as the project moves through its various stages. The project must have a tangible and measurable outcome, and it must be broken down into a sequence of tasks that can be scheduled and controlled.

The advantages of the technique in strategy implementation derive from the disciplines and procedures that have been developed, its multidisciplinary approach, and the measurability of the outputs. Not all the changes that are required to successfully implement a strategy can be managed in this way, but if the basic disciplines of project management can be introduced into the organization, then the more that can be managed through those processes, the greater the likelihood that significant strategic changes can be effected.

Cross-functional teams

As was argued in Chapter 5, every structure is a compromise: if you organize by function you reap the advantages flowing from specialist expertise, but you may suffer from a weak client, product or market focus. Cross-functional teams can be used to overcome some of the disadvantages of functional structures. However, if cross-functional teams are to work they must be managed in the right way, as follows:

◆ They require clear, broad, stable but challenging goals or missions.

◆ They need to be left alone.

◆ They must have "heavyweight" leaders with influence.

◆ The work of teams may need to be coordinated.

◆ The members of the team must be able to deliver the function they represent: that is, they must be powerful enough to make decisions that commit their function.

◆ Team contributions must be recognized and rewarded by functional bosses.

◆ Each team must be stable in order to allow its members to establish good working relationships and develop a team spirit.

Reorganizing the structure

If any of the three processes described above are used, there may well come a point where the old functional groupings and specializations are increasingly inappropriate for the changing direction of the organization. At some point, the logic of the old structure becomes untenable as more and more activity is driven by projects and cross-functional teams in pursuit of the required capabilities. The opportunity may present itself to acknowledge the fundamental shift in the focus of the organization by bringing the formal structure more into line with the actual work of the organization.

We can see this happening in small ways with the development of new specializations such as quality assurance, innovation, technology development, and project and programme management. It may be beneficial to anticipate the evolution of new bases of specialization by proactively reshaping the organization. If it is clear that, in order to gain sustainable advantage, the firm must develop outstanding capabilities – for example, in new product introductions, lowest delivered costs, "right first time" quality, or continual learning – there may be an advantage in recognizing this formally by establishing groups that have as their *primary responsibility* the achievement of these capabilities. This type of bold initiative can be extremely powerful in signalling a major shift in strategic direction.

Identifying barriers to change

A clear sense of strategic direction set out in a good mission statement can be used to help identify the potential barriers to change in the organization. One way of exploring these barriers is to examine the extent to which the current organization supports or constrains movement towards the aims set out in the mission statement. The required capabilities can be derived from brainstorming and grouping the actions needed to fulfil the aims of the statement. The organizational structures, processes and types of information necessary to deliver the required capabilities can be explored. This should highlight the need for new systems and information, and there may also be a demand for new specializations and different groupings. The more intangible aspects of culture can then be addressed by focusing on the values and management styles that are supportive of the mission.

Thus a picture can be developed of the way the organization might need to look if it is to achieve the mission successfully. This vision of a future organization can be used to compare and contrast the present situation. To do this a "force field" approach can be useful. In Figure 7.2 the future organization is represented by the dotted wavy line and the

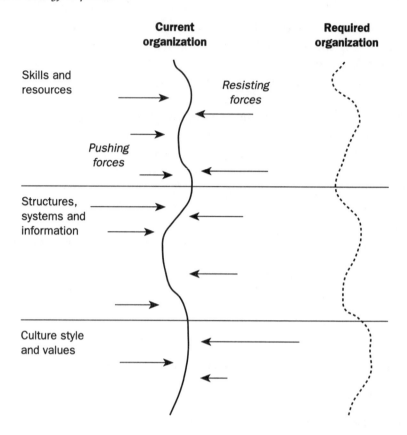

Figure 7.2 *Force-field analysis*

current situation by the solid wavy line. There are forces acting in the organization that are already moving the firm in the right direction: for example, it is already engaged in extensive training in quality assurance, and shop-floor attitudes seem to be in favour of some changes.

However, set against these pushing forces are resisting forces, or barriers to change. To expose these barriers, the management team members will have to engage in some challenging thinking, and they will need to be very open, honest and explicit. If a major barrier is the cynical attitude of the finance director towards any new initiatives, then this issue must be raised and confronted; if the autocratic chief execu-tive is seen to be stifling initiatives, then this too must be brought out into the open and discussed. Not all barriers will be of this sensitive nature, but they may nevertheless be difficult to identify. As argued in the previous chapter, routines dominate organizational behaviour. Ways must be found to isolate and evaluate routine ways of doing things.

Once the relevant pushing and resisting forces have been identified, they can be rated according to their perceived strength or importance. This rating can be represented on the chart by the length of the arrow, as shown in Figure 7.2.

The pace of movement towards the required organization can be increased by *strengthening* the pushing forces, *adding new* pushing forces (e.g. setting up a new product development task force to explore ways of reducing the time to market), or by *reducing* the resisting forces (e.g. firing the finance director). In this way, tangible actions can be identified – by getting managers to think creatively – and these actions, taken together, will accelerate progress towards the aims of the mission statement.

Prioritizing and ownership

Senior managers are busy people. Even if they are supposed to be spending their days managing the strategy of the organization, the chances are that they may well be bogged down in day-to-day operational activities. The management group has, therefore, a limited capacity to do new things, to drive new initiatives. This scarce resource must therefore be deployed to best advantage.

The actions derived from the processes described above must be *prioritized*. This can be done in a systematic way by identifying which actions impinge on the achievement of more than one competence, and then by rating how well this is currently performed. Alternatively, the managers could agree on a subset of actions to be tackled first, this selection to be guided by the following principles:

1. *Select actions that can be accomplished fairly easily, since early success is vital* If there is demonstrable success in tackling an action, this can encourage others to try new ways of doing things, and the momentum of change can be built up.

2. *Select an action that has powerful symbolic qualities* Do something that clearly signals to people that things are changing, and that the organization is breaking away from the past.

7.2 **Leaders and culture**

Illustration

Bob Galvin, chairman of the company, started visiting customers to learn about their quality perspective of Motorola's products. Instead of visiting top management, he met with the people who dealt with Motorola's invoices, and the customers' employees who received, stored and used Motorola's products in the factory. He quickly learned that there were ample opportunities for improvement and that many quality problems needed urgently to be addressed. By communicating his observations in meetings, and through company cases, some of which were distributed by video, he helped to create a sense of urgency that changed people's attitudes and behaviour towards quality improvement.

(Source: *Long Range Planning*, vol. 27 (October 1994).)

Illustration 7.2 explains how Bob Galvin, chairman of Motorola, acted symbolically to address quality problems.

Each prioritized action must be owned by an individual, preferably a volunteer. Collective responsibility rarely works: a particular person must feel accountable for delivering the action. This is necessary in order to encourage busy managers to find the time to work on the things that need changing. Without this accountability the day-to-day demands of the job will drive out the good intentions of the managers. Managers must be accountable, but this does not necessarily mean that they are personally responsible for effecting the actions: instigators of the action may convene small teams from within their departments or from across the organization to implement the required actions.

There must be an agreed timetable of deadlines for the achievement of each action, and managers must be held to account for progress towards the required results. There is some merit in periodically reviewing the strategy implementation process. This review should seek to confirm the broad strategic direction set out in the mission statement, and managers should share their experiences of trying to implement the required changes. They may identify some common barriers to change that may require new actions to be mounted. Sharing the experiences of implementation successes can help others to formulate ideas, and should boost morale.

Lastly, it is important that the control and reward systems reflect the intentions of the mission statement. There is little point in having a mission statement that says "We aim to delight our customers" if there is no genuine attempt to measure the firm's performance against this objective. If the control systems still emphasize other variables (e.g. capacity utilization, overhead recovery, gross margin), then staff will direct their efforts towards these measures, and not towards achieving "delighted customers". To take another example, if the mission statement says, "We aim to have an organization that our staff can be proud of", then this must be brought about in some way. First, managers need to know what would make the staff proud to work there. Secondly, they have to set about changing things so that the staff do become proud of their organization, as well as finding ways (e.g. staff surveys) of measuring how well they are meeting this important aim.

Similarly, rewards must be in tune with the intentions set out in the mission statement. Staff must be recognized and rewarded for behaviour that is clearly in line with the statement: if an employee stays on late to solve a customer's problem, this must be recognized; if a group of people use their initiative to come up with a way of achieving significant savings in material costs they should be appropriately rewarded. It is important to shift the organization away from a conservative, toe-the-line, keep-your-nose-clean culture to one where people are free to experiment, take risks and assume responsibility. Therefore, it is vital that individuals displaying these qualities are encouraged and promoted.

A problem caused by delayering, and exacerbated by the increasing use of part-time and short-term contracted staff, is that the traditional means of motivating people – the prospect of a career in the firm – has been removed for many staff. We need to explore alternatives to the career ladder if we are to stimulate and retain good staff. It may be that more imaginative contracts need to be evolved which recognize that the individual's tenure in the organization may be limited. Perhaps the contract with some staff will involve continual development of their capabilities so that when they leave they are more marketable.

I have deliberately concentrated our attention in this chapter on the most difficult aspects of managing strategic change. These involve changes that require members of an organization to behave in different ways, learn new things, evolve new attitudes. However, it must be recognized that there is another category of strategic change that is essentially about eliminating or reducing aspects of the business: for example, closing an inefficient plant, sacking a layer of management, halving the range of products, withdrawing from unprofitable client relationships, eliminating a shift, or closing the research department.

Such changes may well be painful for the individuals directly affected, and they are of a quite different nature from changes that are concerned with building new capabilities. There is no doubt that dramatic changes can be effected rapidly by sacking people or stripping out activities from the organization, and that radical changes of this nature can have a powerful influence on the attitudes and behaviour of those that remain. Yet when compared with the problems of building capabilities, these draconian changes are fairly straightforward to implement. However, as we pointed out in earlier chapters, if "cutting" is easy to implement, it cannot be a source of competitive advantage, since it can be imitated. Moreover, because of the relatively straightforward nature of cutting strategies, they can be regarded as dominant strategies. If building is vague and ambiguous, the clearer "cutting" strategy will prevail.

A simple model of change, attributed to Gleicher, helps us understand some of the issues involved. If we take as a starting point that there is usually a degree of inertia in an organization, what prompts significant change? Gleicher's model can be set out out follows:

$$\text{Dissatisfaction with status quo} \times \text{Vision} \times \text{First steps} > \text{Costs}$$

The model is multiplicative. No change will occur if any of the items to the left of the sign ($>$) are zero. First, therefore, before change happens there has to be a sufficient critical mass of senior people dissatisfied with the way things are at present and wanting to do something about it. Second, they need to have some vision of where to take the organization. Third, they need to have some understandable first steps to implement, to start the process of change. And the total of all of these multiplied together must exceed the perceived costs of changing. So, there is little point in having a great strategy, and even to have set out in some detail an implementation programme, if no one at the top is sufficiently dissatisfied with the way things are at present. In this case nothing will happen.

Nonetheless, even where an individual executive feels dissatisfied with the status quo, and he or she has a vision, and some obvious first steps suggest themselves, they may still feel that they lack the self-confidence to take action.

Building experience and self-confidence

Belief and confidence

From the perspective of an individual executive (say, the CEO), strategic change in general would be viewed as a risky venture. Disturbing the status quo, the ongoing routines of the organization, should not be undertaken lightly. The adage "If it ain't broke, don't fix it" cautions us against taking any actions that might inadvertently interfere with the vital organs of the firm. However, one circumstance where we might feel more comfortable about taking action is when we perceive we are in a crisis. The sense of crisis is strangely liberating: "Hell, we're all going down the tubes, anyway, so we might as well try something." The shared sense of crisis allows us to take actions that would previously have been considered too risky.

As I have argued, in most firms the crisis is dealt with by implementing well-understood generic cost-cutting recipes: budgets are slashed, layers eliminated, plants closed, product lines trimmed. These actions can be taken confidently: the solutions are ready-made and well understood, while the need to take action is justified by the shared sense of crisis. Executives can behave strategically in these circumstances with some degree of self-confidence.

Where does this self-confidence come from? In the case of the "crisis leading to cuts" strategic response, executives can draw on their own past experiences of previous crises, in this and other organizations, and they can also gain strength from a collective managerial understanding that this is normal management behaviour. Indeed, to respond in any other way may be seen as a sign of weakness.

Change without crisis

But crises are special circumstances. Does strategic change occur without a performance deterioration? It does, of course, but here the executive does not have the legitimizing context of a crisis to help him or her. So where does the confidence to change come from when there is no sense of crisis?

Strategic changes can come about when a new CEO is appointed. The self-confidence to challenge the status quo derives from the new CEO's past experiences. Often he or she is merely implementing a formula or recipe from their previous organization. The CEO knows this works, because he or she has seen it in action.

Similarly, changes occur when a firm is taken over. Here, the confidence to change is a collective confidence, born out of shared experience of the corporate recipe, and embedded in set of "post-takeover" corporate routines. This is a "trick" we know how to work, and we know it works because we have experienced its implementation in other organizations we have acquired.

Understanding strategic detail

Confidence to change existing routines and structures stems from successful experience of the recipe or formula. The more personal experience the executive has of the recipe, the higher the level of confidence he or she will have in it. So changes I invented, implemented and saw were successful, have built in me an unshakeable belief in the recipe. This self-confidence has enabled me to drive through difficult change, to sustain momentum and not to be deflected from the imposition of my vision.

Lower levels of belief are generated by personal experience of being *involved* in the recipe, as recipient rather than instigator. For example, if I moved from my current school, judged to be one of the top schools in the country, to a lesser ranked school, I would understand what a good school should look like, and, hopefully, be able to make some changes to my new organization in line with this vision. But although I understand how a good school looks and feels, I do not necessarily understand *how this comes about.* Thus there is some know-how that eludes me; possibly some of the founders of the school have it, or perhaps no one does, as these causes of success are embedded in the implicit routines and shared values of the school. The knowledge is tacit.

However, as I have personal experience of the recipe, I understand, maybe implicitly, a great deal of richness and detail about the nature of this successful organization. I know how it feels to work in it, I understand the style of interactions between faculty and with our clients, I appreciate what would be acceptable and unacceptable behaviour, and so on. I thus have intimate experience of the recipe at a very detailed level: I understand it at the level of basic organizational routines.

Let us consider another context of change, the circumstance facing, say, our lower-ranked school. The new dean, appointed from *within* the ranks of the faculty, sees it as her role to lift the school into the top five nationally. The strategy for change is to mimic and replicate what the top schools do. She visits the top schools to see how it is done, and persuades the university to cede extra cash, to fund more research, to recruit new staff, to refurbish the buildings, and so on.

The problem here, however, is that she does not have personal experience of the recipe to draw on. This can place the new dean in a vulnerable position if things start to go wrong. If you do not understand the detail of the recipe, you are less able to make judgements about the appropriateness or otherwise of the unfolding changes.

This is a considerable problem with the adoption of any "off-the-shelf" strategic solution, whether it be business process re-engineering, "cost leadership", or total quality. If you, as the instigator of the change, only understand the *principles* of the change, and not its detailed routines, then the chances are that you will not have the level of belief to drive the changes through. This is why consultants are picking up business by selling their expertise in implementation: they understand the recipe in *principle* and, through experience of implementation in other contexts, they understand it in *detail* too.

This would suggest that in order for an organization to undertake a successful strategic change, someone in the organization must have had personal experience of the process and its desired result. Without this level of experience, no one individual possesses sufficient understanding of the required state to generate the necessary level of belief in it. When problems of implementation are encountered, therefore, the lack of belief leads to us abandoning the change, or severely curtailing its impact.

Real strategic change is felt in the fundamental routines of the organization. Thus, if change is to happen, it is at this very basic level that it has to take place. This requires an understanding of the detail of the change. Can this be generated inside the organization?

Where the change can be practised, rehearsed or piloted in some way, managers can then understand at least some of the practical details of the change. A pilot scheme can also highlight problems and unforeseen consequences. A successful pilot scheme will also start to build confidence and belief in the change, as well as providing a tangible symbol to others. In the same context, if we can identify pockets of the organization where new developments are taking place spontaneously (e.g. better working arrangements are being explored) or where morale and performance levels seem to be well above average, we can try to learn from these "experiments". Because these experiments are already happening, it is possible to understand the *detail* of the innovation, which should make it easier to implement or replicate it elsewhere. The next stage would presumably be to *promote* the process of innovation by encouraging experiments throughout the organization. Clearly, resources would have to be made available to facilitate these experiments, and ultimately these rather informal experiments should become an integral part of the culture.

We can now be more specific in defining "strategy". I believe that a sense of strategy means *knowing what to change in the organization, and, more importantly, knowing what to change it to*. This also means that we need to understand what should *not* change. In this respect, concern for the *strategic detail* of the firm is vital, to make sure that we do not inadvertently interfere with a source of advantage. We can act more confidently in changing aspects of the organization if we really understand, at the level of routines and individuals, those activities and behaviours that confer advantage.

So what?

In this chapter we have focused on the practical issues involved in managing strategic change. Hence some of the "So what?" questions that might be posed had a more theoretical treatment been adopted, probably do not apply. However, here are some observations that either reinforce or augment some of the points made in the chapter:

◆ Commitment to change stems from *belief* in the *need* for change and in the *path* to be followed. Self-confidence in what to change things *to* often derives from an individual's personal experience of the "solution" in another context. And belief in the need for change is often generated by a sense of crisis. Some corporate leaders have understood this and they try to instil an almost permanent sense of crisis in the subsidiary businesses they control through the setting of performance targets that are almost impossible to achieve.

♦ In the absence of a perceived crisis to provoke change, and where there is no ready-made strategic recipe or solution to hand that can be easily adopted, a top team can comfortably avoid addressing the firm's strategic agenda.

♦ Belief and confidence in a new strategy can be generated internally by a team through thorough and open debate, supported by good analysis based upon decent information. To reduce the perceived risks of changing the routines of the organization, wherever possible the change should be pilot-tested in a small way. This can help to flesh out the important details of the change, and the visible evidence that the new, future organization could actually work gives managers and staff alike more confidence in the strategy.

♦ Resistance to change is often exaggerated. Frequently, anticipated resistance makes executives behave in ways which actually *provoke* resistance: they try to keep the changes a secret, which encourages rumours, which alerts staff, who, in consequence, take the least optimistic view of the likely effects of the anticipated changes on themselves – so they resist!

♦ Weak signals that offer advanced warning of the need to change can be down-played, reinterpreted, or simply ignored by executives. To avoid this, many staff, particularly those in regular contact with buyers, channels, and competitors, should be used as listening posts, and their opinions and intuitive judgements about the firm's situation should be heeded.

♦ The longest journey starts with a single step, and in selecting which first step to take, bear in mind the symbolic importance of some actions and the need to achieve an early success.

♦ I am often asked why I focus so much attention on the top team, and the need for them to be committed to change. Some argue for "bottom up" change, rather than the "top down" approach I tend to assume. Experience tells me that unless the CEO is committed to change, nothing much happens. It certainly helps if a critical power group in the upper echelons of the organization also support the change, and of course, the project gains tremendous impetus if staff all the way down the hierarchy back the new strategy.

Realistically, however, change is likely to cause a degree of anxiety: some may find themselves out of a job, and a few will leave because they cannot cope with the demands of their new roles. To drive changes which have these consequences requires a tough stance from the very top. So the first problem is to persuade the CEO to act, then the top team, and so on down the structure.

◆ If belief and commitment stems from genuine involvement in the strategy-making process, a process of cascading the strategy should be adopted, whereby each level down in the structure is given some scope in working through the details of the strategy. For example, at corporate level, ambitious targets might be set for strategic business units (SBUs), but the SBU management are given scope to decide strategies for achieving these targets; the CEO of the SBU then sets the broad agenda for change; the top executive team debate and discuss strategic options and agree a broad strategy; this strategy is passed to the next level of functional managers, who are not able to challenge the broad thrust of the strategy, but are allowed to determine their function's response to this new direction; and so on down the hierarchy. Nonetheless, in formulating the broad strategy, while the top team may consult with various management levels below them, ultimately it is that team's responsibility to set the strategic direction for the SBU.

Summary

Strategic change has to be considered from a cultural perspective. We suggested that piecemeal changes may be too easily absorbed into the existing culture, leading to no real change. We then went on to argue that the strategy process itself can critically affect the chances of any change occurring, particularly if the process does not generate top-level commitment. We explored a likely sequence in a change process, which is often triggered by a sense of crisis. Prescriptions were proferred that can assist change processes, which included mission statements, competence champions, project management, and the use of cross-functional teams. We showed how barriers to change can be represented using force-field analysis. Finally, we looked at change from the perspective of the individual executive, focusing on the importance of generating belief and self-confidence in the change.

CHAPTER 8

Corporate strategy

Corporate strategy addresses the questions: "Which businesses should we be in, and how should we run them?" The main areas of corporate strategy may be summarized as *selecting*, *resourcing* and *controlling* the businesses within the corporation. Above all, the corporate strategy needs to identify how and where the corporate centre will add value, both by what it does well, and by how it is able to assist the business units to achieve a higher performance within the corporation than they could alone.

Creating value from the centre

The corporate centre can provide value in its direct actions, over and above its primary tasks of selecting, resourcing, and controlling the strategic business units (SBUs). It can identify and develop the core competences that bind the business units together, and/or it can exercise certain competences directly itself. For example, an industrial corporation identifies the following competences as being common across all its SBUs:

- Problem-solving, rather than just selling products.

- Building long-term relationships.

- Being sensitive to global/local response to market demand.

Such competences are corporatewide: that is, insofar as SBUs in the corporation in question are expected to have them in large measure, and the absence of these competences in a particular SBU would raise questions regarding the continued presence of that SBU in the group.

However, there are other competences that may be present and be value-enhancing in the corporate centre itself. For example, the ability to identify businesses that are undervalued on the stock market; competences in implementing tight financial and budgetary controls; a culture that encourages innovation – these may all be competences at the corporate level that can add value. But, using the same arguments we developed for competitive strategy, in order for these competences to be a source of sustained corporate advantage, they would have to be difficult to imitate.

In their *Corporate Level Strategy* (Wiley, 1994), Goold, Campbell and Alexander talk of corporate "parenting". They argue that there are four broad ways in which the corporate parent can add value to the SBUs under its control:

1. *Stand alone influence* The parent enhances the stand-alone performance of the SBU.

2. *Linkage influence* The parent enhances the value of linkages *between* the SBUs.

3. *Functional and service influence* The parent provides functional leadership and cost-effective services for the business units.

4. *Corporate development activities* Here, the parent creates value by altering the composition of the portfolio of business units.

There are therefore different ways in which the corporate centre can add value. Once it is clear what the role of the centre is in adding value, the relationship between the centre and the SBUs should become much clearer. For example, if the parent is adding value through "linkage influence", we would expect the corporate centre to be actively engaged in fostering connections between SBUs, assisting the transfer of know-how across units, encouraging common procurement policies, and so on.

Selecting: should we diversify?

The fourth parenting role is concerned with the selection of business units. The selecting task of the corporation involves deciding whether to go into a new market or to develop a new set of competences. Venturing beyond known market boundaries and competences involves increasing risk. However, a strategy to continue operating in the existing product/ market segment with existing competences may not achieve acceptable results. The market may be saturated, or the competences may be obsolete or at least in decline. In what follows, *four* possible diversification options are set out.

Generally, the lowest risk option is *staying with existing competences that are adapted to current markets*. Once the corporation moves away from this position, the risks increase. Where new markets are explored with existing competences, the risks stem from the relative unfamiliarity of the environment. We may also be unsure about the appropriateness of our existing competences in this new arena. How transferable are they? Can we be sure we can match the competences of incumbent firms? We saw in Chapter 3 the importance of strategic detail, and how a generic competence in, say, procurement may not give advantage in a market where the firm is up against more experienced rivals. Illustration 8.1 summarizes some of the motives for diversifying.

Acquiring or *developing new competences to improve our performance in current markets* involves internal risks. There are risks whether we acquire the competence externally by buying a business that has it, or whether we try to develop this capability ourselves. The riskiest option is trying to apply new competences to new markets: in this case, there

8.1 Motives for diversification

Illustration

Why are companies drawn to diversification? I think they're drawn to it for a number of reasons. They want to grow, and they can only grow so much in their basic business. They want to deploy excess resources, have cash, manpower, reputation, images that can be used elsewhere, that are underutilized in the core business. I also think that any discussion of diversification is ultimately going to miss part of the point if we don't recognize that there is a big chunk of ego and glamour involved in diversification. If you look at the covers of the major business publications, one of the best ways of getting on the cover is through diversification, at least that's what history tells us. I think the excitement of the chase in buying and selling is awfully invigorating to many managers.

The key to thinking about diversification is actually very simple, but often forgotten. It is that diversification makes no sense unless the corporation, if you will, adds value. This means that being part of a corporation actually makes the units in individual businesses better off.

(Source: Extract from "Michael Porter on competitive strategy reflections and round table discussion", *European Management Journal*, vol. 6, 1 (1987).)

is no familiar ground, and little prospect of success. It may be that a corporation would only be forced into this position in a state of crisis, otherwise it is difficult to see how the corporation can add value through this move.

A corporation's initial concern, therefore, must be to achieve the strongest possible position, using its existing proven competences in existing markets. If this gives inadequate results, however, the corporation will need to consider the higher risk options of *moving to different markets*, and/or possibly *developing different competences*. These moves involve still higher risk, since they mean moving into unfamiliar territory.

Resourcing

How do we develop?

The question of whether to make the moves *by internal development, by alliance* or *by acquisition* has to be considered, since, with the exception of internal development, all moves involve the unfamiliar, and thus raise the company's risk.

Internal development usually incurs least risk, as it has the greatest level of control and familiarity with the firm's existing competences. However, if this option is not possible – perhaps for reasons of resource deficiency, or the need for speed in launching a new product in order to meet an opportunity without having appropriate internal competences to do this – the riskier options of alliance or acquisition must be considered.

Some form of alliance with a partner overcomes many of the problems stemming from lack of resources and competences. New products from one company can be married to sales forces from another company who have spare capacity, and the time from product to market can be dramatically shortened. Companies strong on technology can collaborate with partners who are excellent at marketing, to their mutual benefit. The wide variety of joint-development formats provides a menu of possibilities for partners to select from in order to optimize their development possibilities. Joint development is appropriate where sustainable competitive advantage can be achieved together, but not

separately. Through such an alliance, a weak competence can be transformed by the addition of the partner's core competences.

The make/buy/ally matrix

The competence of the company in particular activities is an influence
in determining the boundary of a particular corporation. The make/buy/
ally matrix, set out by Bowman and Faulkner in their *Competitive and
Corporate Strategy* (Irwin, 1997), and illustrated in Figure 8.1, helps a
company's management to determine how best it should carry out
particular activities. The horizontal axis measures dimensions of the
relative competences of firms needing to carry out specific activities,
and the vertical axis measures the strategic importance of particular
activities to the competitive success of those firms.

All companies, even the largest, have scarce resources, so it is not
making the best use of those resources to direct them at activities which
are not strategically significant. Very few companies make their own
travel arrangements, for example: they subcontract them to a travel
company who can then take advantage of scale economies and the

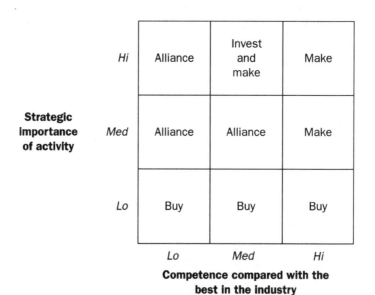

Figure 8.1 *The make/buy/ally matrix*

experience curve to provide a better and cheaper service. Thus, if the activity is of little strategic significance to the company it should be bought in, because even though the company might be very proficient at that activity, carrying it out personally is not making the best use of scarce resources. If, however, the activity is strategically in the range of fairly to very significant, and the company carries it out very well, this activity should be performed internally. At the same time, if the activity is very strategically significant, but the company performs it only passably, the company should invest to improve its performance in that activity. However, should the company's performance at a strategically significant activity be only moderate at best, an alliance may be required to enable the company to learn the necessary skills that will improve its performance.

The operational value of the above schema depends on how accurately it is possible to measure strategic significance and efficiency of performance. Efficiency is the easier to measure; measuring strategic significance is more difficult.

On the question of strategic significance, perhaps the key measure is whether the activity is important to the achievement of competitive advantage. Hence a computer hardware company that subcontracts *all* its manufacture is taking a large strategic risk, as it is consigning the production of items upon which its reputation depends to companies it does not control. For a firm like Reebok, on the other hand, where the company is basically a development and marketing company, the risk is less, since the competitive advantage lies in product innovation and brand marketing.

Illustration 8.2 explains how companies are collaborating by using alliances and partnerships to acquire and develop the competences required to compete in the biotechnology and pharmaceutical industries. Clearly, in order to benefit from these arrangements, skills must be developed in the *management* of alliance relationships.

Vertical and horizontal integration

The make/buy/ally matrix provides pointers to which activities should be performed internally, and which consigned to the market. However, it does not deal with the relationship between competences, and the economies of scale and scope available in the performance of one or a range of activities.

8.2 Strategic alliances in the pharmaceutical industry

Illustration

Fresh sciences give opportunities for reducing costs and cutting trial times.

Three new technologies are coming together to transform research in the biotechnology and pharmaceutical industries: genomics, combinatorial chemistry, and high-throughput screening. And underlying all three is informatics, the application of computing power to biological and chemical information.

There are two broad reasons why companies are investing in these technologies. First, they hope to generate better treatments for diseases for which current drugs are ineffective and/or afflicted with serious side-effects. Secondly, they want to cut the costs and time taken to produce potential drugs for clinical trials.

In order to remain competitive, all the integrated drug companies have had to build up expertise in all three technologies – both in-house and through webs of alliances with specialist biotech companies and academic research groups.

The three technologies form a "value chain": genomics companies are most valuable, followed by combinatorial chemistry companies, and then screening specialists.

Information about the 100,000 human genes is the most expensive to obtain, has the greatest scarcity value, and is most useful for drug discovery. Biotech companies focusing on genomics include Human Genome Sciences, Millennium, Sequana, Incyte, Myriad, Lynx and Genset.

Best known is Human Genome Sciences, based in Maryland, which formed a far-reaching partnership with SmithKline Beecham, the Anglo-American pharmaceutical giant, in 1993. This has thrown up far more genomic information than the original partners can use themselves – even though George Poste, SB's head of R & D, says almost all his company's new drugs will be based on the HGS alliance – so it has been extended to take in four more drug companies: Schering Plough of the US, Merck of Germany, Synthelabo of France and Takeda of Japan.

Genetics Institute, based in Massachusetts, recently announced a collaboration with two prominent Californian biotech companies, Chiron and Genentech, to identify and characterize the functions of "secreted proteins". GI says its Discover-Ease technology has already identified genes for 5,000 secreted proteins.

Many small companies are specializing in helping pharmaceutical and biotechnology groups to automate combinatorial chemistry and link it to high-throughput screening. For example, the Technology Partnership, a UK consultancy based near Cambridge, has a consortium of drug companies – including Merck of the US, Pfizer, Takeda, BASF, Ciba, SmithKline Beecham and Chiroscience – using its Myriad automated synthesis system.

(Source: *Financial Times*, 26 November 1996.)

If many products are best produced in companies, which activities should the company carry out, and why should there be any limit to the size of a company? The answer to these questions is found primarily in the shape of the firm's cost curve, and the limits to the degree of economies of scale and scope that exist, after which the diseconomies of bureaucracy begin to cause the curve to bend upwards. When this point is reached, it becomes more efficient to operate in a smaller company, or to buy in more activities, and to restrict the company's activities to those in which it excels and which give it its competitive advantage.

The arguments in favour of vertical integration are that activities involving proprietorial technologies, and activities requiring high levels of coordination, lead to more reliable performance if they are carried out within the firm. As volume grows, the experience curve enables costs to be lowered, and scale and scope economies strengthen the cost reduction movement even further. With integrated manufacture, quality control is also easier to ensure, and the risks of opportunism at the transfer stages are substantially reduced.

On the other side of the argument, though, are the following considerations. Vertical integration removes the market discipline at each transfer interface, and therefore is likely to lead to inefficiency, and the reverse of "lean production". Each stage in the production process involves manufacturing only sufficient volume for the end product's requirements. This is likely to result in suboptimal production volumes in relation to maximizing scale economies. An integrated firm loses flexibility and can become locked into old technologies, whereas a subcontracting firm can switch suppliers more easily. Furthermore, firms that buy parts in the market economize on the use of capital, reduce the overall level of risk, and can, if they choose suppliers carefully, take advantage of expert specialist production without having to go to the time and expense of learning the specialisms. The arguments for and against vertical integration are therefore finely balanced and can only be resolved on a case-by-case basis.

Horizontal integration – that is, integrating activities with those of a competitor through merger, acquisition or partnership – is easier to assess. Providing it enables the firm to take optimal advantage of the opportunities presented by the existence of potential economies of scale and scope, horizontal integration is appropriate. Clearly, where buying your competitor involves operating two suboptimal-sized factories and two overlapping sales forces, then the argument for horizontal integration is not made. Conversely, should it enable you to achieve your maximum economic production size in one factory, the cost argument for horizontal integration is strong. The recent merger of Sun Alliance with Royal Insurance would be an example where significant economies of scale and scope were anticipated. Also, of course, where there are few firms in the industry, a merger between two major players can reduce the competitive element. The EU's political involvement in the marriage of Boeing with McDonnell Douglas derives from this concern.

Selecting and resourcing: mergers and acquisitions

An acquisition or merger is an alternative way of providing resources to that of internal development. However, an acquisition of a company which the acquirer knows little about prior to the bid, is the highest-risk method of providing resources that the corporation can adopt. As a means of implementing a competitive strategy, it is generally pursued to gain access to core competences in which the acquiring company feels itself to be deficient and which will enable it to compete successfully in a particular market. The hope is that the two companies, which individually may lack competitive advantage in their chosen market, will achieve that advantage together.

There are other reasons of corporate strategy for undertaking acquisitions: for example, restructuring the market, achieving a more ''balanced'' portfolio of businesses, gaining access to advantageous tax losses, building a bigger empire, or achieving corporate growth targets at times when development through organic growth proves difficult. It is the combining of resources and skills, however, in order to achieve competitive advantage that *should* be the primary strategic reason for making an acquisition.

Acquisitions, particularly those involving large publicly quoted companies, probably attract more attention in the media than any other aspect of business life, except perhaps scandals involving prominent personalities. Yet, in the real world of acquisitions there are several enigmas which suggest that the process described above may not always lead to beneficial results for all parties concerned.

First, premiums in excess of 30 per cent are quite commonly found, particularly in the case of contested bids. But why are such high premiums so often paid by the bidder if the takeover target is correctly valued by the stock market in the first place? The justification for this can only be that the incoming management recognizes ways of either adding value through synergies or removing the sources of inefficiency, or both. Secondly, if the main justification for acquisitions is the existence of potential synergies between the acquirer and the target, why are these synergies apparently so seldom realized? Thirdly, if the acquisition is an efficiency-enhancing mechanism, why are there clearly discernible waves of merger/acquisition activity (e.g. the early 1970s and the middle and late 1980s)? Finally, if acquisitions are generally promoted by the bidding company because they can be seen to lead to potential gains for at least one of the parties involved, why do the figures suggest that the gainers are most frequently the shareholders of the "victim" company (i.e. the one that is acquired), while the shareholders of the bidder company and the management of the victim company are more often the losers?

So why acquire?

Acquisition has some theoretical advantages over both internal development and alliances that make it a popular strategy for an ambitious company intent on fast growth, as follows:

- ◆ Acquisition enables a firm to gain entry rapidly into new market or product areas.

- ◆ It may enable costs to be reduced through rationalization and the consequent economies of scale and of scope to be realized.

- ◆ It may bring valuable skills and resources to the acquiring company, thereby strengthening its core competences and improving its competitive position.

- ◆ By acquiring a competitor, the company may improve its market share and put itself in a stronger market position.

- ◆ By acquiring a company either upstream or downstream in its value system, a firm may reduce costs at the interface between activities.

These arguments are, however, largely theoretical and sometimes difficult to substantiate.

There are other arguments and motives which are less theoretical. For instance:

- ◆ Takeover bids are generally mounted by the management rather than the shareholders of the bidding company. Whatever the results for the shareholders may be, it is rare for the new managers of the enlarged enterprise not to benefit by a substantial salary increase and possibly share options.

- ◆ A further argument is that firms with free cash flow who are finding organic growth difficult prefer acquisitions to the alternative of returning the cash to the shareholders. This is a variant on the "empire building" argument for expansion by acquisition.

- ◆ Once it is conceded that the stock market is a less than perfect mechanism for valuing companies, motives for acquisitions become clearer. Thus if the bidding company has superior information it may recognize a bargain which the stock market is unaware of. It may also for reasons of fashion have a very high price/earnings ratio not really justified by the firm's genuine long-term prospects. In this case, to use the high P/E and buy with "paper" (i.e. its own overvalued shares) represents a rational decision and a certain way of increasing shareholder value, at least in the short-term.

- ◆ A further motive for acquisitions is to diversify risk, or to iron out seasonal variations in cash flow. This may give the company more stable earnings which, if the effect is substantial, may lower its cost of borrowing by increasing its credit rating. The history of generally poor performance by conglomerates in the medium term has, however, somewhat discredited this argument.

In general, the acquisition strategy is one that should be employed with great caution. Typically, the more closely related the business of the candidate for acquisition to the business of the acquirer, the smaller is the risk, since the new owner will be familiar with the major problems likely to be encountered and will be experienced in dealing with them. An acquisition of an unfamiliar company in an unrelated area of business from both a market and a product viewpoint is therefore the highest risk strategy of all, and should be resisted if at all possible.

The notable exception to this general rule is when the acquiring company's core competence is in company appraisal, acquisition and financial management (e.g. Hanson). In this case, such a company can legitimately claim to be operating in the area it knows best, even if the products and markets of the company to be acquired are not familiar.

Controlling: achieving synergies

The role of the corporate centre in controlling SBUs should be determined by the overriding logic or rationale for the corporation. Once it is clear, say, that these businesses have been collected together in an attempt to diversify business risks, then the role of the corporate centre reduces to an "arms-length" relationship. A very small corporate HQ focuses on setting return on capital employed (ROCE) targets and monitoring and reviewing SBU performance against these targets.

In contrast, where the corporate logic drives the development of related businesses, so that core competence advantages can be leveraged across similar SBUs, the role of the centre is quite different. Here, corporate staff may be involved in fostering the transfer of staff, systems and learning across related SBUs. And if there is a synergy logic, a substantial range of activities may be performed centrally at corporate HQ (e.g. brand development, R & D, training, procurement).

The corporate centre can therefore identify and help in the achievement of any synergies that may potentially exist between the SBUs, thus aiding in the achievement of economies of scope. The identification and realization of synergies can be an important part of the value added contribution brought about by the corporate centre. The SBU concept upon which the multidivisional form of diversified company organization structure is based works on the assumption that SBUs are largely self-contained businesses. This drives out synergies by definition.

In principle, the opportunity to examine potential synergies arises directly from the acquisition by the corporation of new business units. A newly acquired unit may have a supplier or customer in common with an existing unit, or may allow manufacture with common plant, and so the opportunities unfold.

Marketing synergies may exist through a variety of channels: for example, the spreading of the corporate brand name over a wider range of products; shared advertising and promotion; the use of the same distribution network and sales force for a wider range of product; cross-selling by executives in different SBUs; and sharing the back-office administration associated with the sales and marketing function. Procurement synergies may exist through shared purchasing leading to greater volume discounts, and production synergies through shared production facilities, shared quality systems and shared maintenance departments. "State of the art" technologies may also be located over a range of business units to corporate advantage.

On the negative side, there are of course both financial and motivational costs in attempting to realize synergies between SBUs. On the financial side, there are the costs involved in setting up and maintaining the coordination systems necessary to realize the synergies: for example, the costs of management time, committees, and the compromises that are needed when one SBU is measured by its results and yet is required, in the interest of the corporation as a whole, to take actions that may only benefit another SBU. Motivational costs can also be an important consideration in selecting which synergies to go for. The achievement of intra-SBU synergies inevitably leads to a degree of diffused profit responsibility, loss of focus, reduced flexibility, and a blurring of the cause–effect relationship. It is difficult to know whether you are right to sell off a poorly performing business, when it is intertwined in a complex way with the rest of the corporation, sharing production plant, sales force and perhaps R & D.

Other barriers to the achievement of synergistic benefits include the following:

◆ Usually the costs of achieving synergies are more tangible than the potential benefits, which can discourage managers from pursuing synergies.

◆ There are cultural barriers to cooperation between SBUs,

particularly where firms who were once competitors find themselves forced to collaborate.

◆ The benefits of collaboration between SBUs are likely to be unequally spread. Hence some managements will be less motivated to search for corporate synergies than others.

◆ There may be a strong reluctance to "interfere" with a successful SBU, particularly where the sources of that SBU's success are not fully understood.

Illustration 8.3 explains how ABB, a successful multinational corporation, has used matrix structure to help its constituent businesses gain synergistic benefits from being part of a larger corporation, while at the same time allowing firms to be responsive to their local markets.

Strategy problems in not-for-profit organizations

This book has concentrated on firms and corporations operating in competitive markets. However, there are many organizations that do not fit these circumstances: public service organizations, charities, police and armed forces, universities, and so on. These not-for-profit organizations have fundamentally different strategic issues to face compared with private sector firms. At a very basic level, they often do not have a clear objective.

I have taken for granted in this text that firms are striving to make profits. It may be the case that they are not strictly trying to "maximize" profits, but all firms have to make *some* level of profit just to survive. This measurable objective makes life much simpler, if more brutal, in the firm. Strategies can be evaluated using this yardstick, and activities and even individuals can be assessed according to their contribution to this "bottom line".

Strategy in not-for-profit organizations is, by contrast, not at all straightforward. Usually there are different groups with differing views about the purpose of the organization. Rarely do they have a measurable objective, and often their mission can change over time as the power of various pressure groups waxes and wanes. These organizations tend to be highly politicized, and the lack of clarity of purpose therefore engenders political battles over resources and priorities.

Illustration

8.3 Matrix system helps local companies "think global, act local"

ABB is organized into a "flat" structure with relatively few layers of management between the CEO and workers on the shop floor. This results in improved communication and allows for greater company involvement with customers – a formula that many of today's management experts tout as vital to future productivity.

President and CEO Percy Barnevik, his deputy CEO, and eleven vice-presidents sit on ABB's executive committee. Meeting every three weeks, the group is responsible for devising ABB's global strategy and monitoring performance. These vice-presidents oversee eight "business segments" representing the company's products and services – power plants, power transmission, power distribution, industry, transportation, environmental control, financial services, and "various activities". These segments, in turn, are composed of fifty major "business areas" (BAs).

The power plants segment, for instance, includes such BAs as gas, steam, and nuclear power plants; the industry group includes instrumentation, process automation, and semiconductors; the transportation group includes mass transit vehicles, rail systems, and main-line rolling stock; and the various activities group includes robotics, power lines and motors.

Each of the fifty BAs has a leader responsible for maximizing that area of business globally. For example, the leader for power transformers, working out of Germany, is responsible for twenty-five factories in sixteen countries. He coordinates overall strategy, allocates export markets to each factory, and oversees cross-training and employee development.

Separate from this distributed network by business area is a geographical country structure consisting of ABB member companies, each having its own president and board of directors. These member companies maintain their own ledger books and are responsible for profits and losses. Within a country, the various local companies are subsidiaries of the member company. Thus presidents of the 1,300 local companies have two bosses: the BA leader and the president of the national member company.

This matrix structure allows local companies to behave like other local companies, that is, to place the interests of local customers – governments, utilities and manufacturers – foremost. The French ABB companies need to be French to succeed, just as the Swiss ABB companies need to understand the needs and interests of the Swiss, Barnevik says. But the other aspect of the matrix – the interconnections with other ABB companies in the business area and group – allow ABB managers to strategically allocate use of resources and production capacity.

(Source: *R&D Magazine*, December 1991.)

I believe, therefore, that strategy is even more critical in these not-for-profit organizations. In the absence of a single measurable objective, the top management must provide a clarity of purpose themselves. It is incumbent on the top team (and on the CEO or equivalent in particular) to reduce ambiguity by establishing some clear sense of purpose. Unfortunately, we cannot use the tools and techniques set out in this book to help a team set such a clear sense of direction in a not-for-profit organization, because the models and frameworks explained in the preceding chapters have been developed with the involvement of executives from the private, profit-oriented sector, rather than from public service organizations.

However, some of these devices have been imaginatively adapted by some of my colleagues to provide some useful perspectives for not-for-profit managers. What is really required, though, is an equivalent range of tools for use with public sector organizations. Those interested in strategy in not-for-profit organizations might care to read chapter 9 in Bowman and Asch's *Managing Strategy* (Macmillan, 1996).

So what?

◆ The fundamental question at corporate level is, "What is the *logic* of the corporation?" In other words, what is the point of collecting all these businesses under one corporate roof? There must be a logic of some sort, and if we are clear what it is, we can then resolve the relationships between the centre and the SBUs, and between SBUs. My fear here is that in some corporations no one has really thought this point through. The lurches in "strategy" that take place periodically in some corporations are, in my view, evidence to support this assertion: for example, we embark on a buying spree, acquire a collection of businesses, only to sell them off at a loss a few years later. The initial logic in these cases was probably "synergy" – the closing logic might be to do with focusing on "core businesses".

◆ Looking at corporate-level strategy from the point of view of an SBU executive, we can pose some challenging questions. In a sense, SBUs pay a *tax* for being in the corporation: they provide the funds through their sales efforts that pay for the corporate-level staff. Managers at SBU level could therefore legitimately ask the question, "What do we get for our money?" More specifically, and perhaps less controversially, SBU managers should pose the questions: How does being part of this corporation help us to compete more effectively? Does it help us to achieve lower unit costs, so that we can be more aggressive on price? Does it help us to add PUV, by, say, leveraging off of the corporate reputation (e.g. as a Virgin Group company benefits from the the brand's reputation and image)?

◆ We should be wary of synergy arguments. If we make a case for an acquisition based on synergies we should be very clear and precise about what form these synergistic benefits will take (i.e exactly how they will help us to cut costs, sell more, innovate faster, and so forth). And we should be explicit about the mechanisms whereby these potential advantages can be realized. How will we cross-sell? How will we centralize training and development?

◆ Alliances are a good way of augmenting the competences of our organization. Typically, however, the problems with alliances stem from the "softer" issues of culture and management commitment. To benefit from alliances requires a new type of corporate level skill, which is not commonly found in traditionally structured hierarchical corporations that are used to a culture of control.

Concluding comments

In the opening chapter I stressed that this was a book about strategy, not planning. What is important is a shared understanding of the strategic direction the business is taking, not the excellence of a planning document. The issues, tools and techniques explained should be used to provoke lively debate. You can never get perfect information, and it is impossible to craft the ideal strategy, because the future is unknown. A more realistic goal, therefore, is to develop some energy and commitment among the team, fashioned around a broad understanding of what we are trying to do with the business. This cannot be a detailed blueprint. There must be some flexibility in the guidelines to allow for unexpected future situations, and to permit levels below the top team some scope to introduce their own ideas and initiatives into the evolving realized strategy.

What cannot be avoided, however, is the top team's responsibility to provide a sense of direction to other staff in the organization. A firm that lacks a shared sense of direction is unlikely to be able to develop sustained advantage, and it will be vulnerable to competitors who are more focused in their intent. Also, levels of management below the top team can easily become demoralized if there are inconsistent messages emanating from the top. Some sense of direction is better than no sense of direction, and, since you cannot derive the perfect strategy, a plan that emerges from a robust debate, fuelled by realistic analyses, should generate a reasonable degree of self-confidence within the team.

Case study: S. J. Matthews

The firm was set up by Saul Matthews in 1947 to supply consumables to catering establishments in Bedfordshire. Consumables in the catering and hotel trade are items like paper napkins, plastic cups, table covers, coasters and doilies, paper plates, and paper towels. The present owner, Steve Whitfield, bought the business off the Matthews family in 1980, in conjunction with 3i. In 1996 Steve purchased the 3i shares to become sole owner. Currently the business is turning over £820,000, with a net profit of £39,000 (see Figure C1.1). Steve believes that the business is underperforming, and he feels he needs some outside perspective brought into his deliberations.

The market

Steve divides the customer base into the following five groups, but SJM only serve three of them:

A *Very small businesses* For example, a chip shop, or a small café. These customers are most likely to use a cash-and-carry warehouse to buy their consumables. SJM do not target these buyers.

B *Local area customers* These are customers in the Bedford area that SJM serve directly. This category includes a wide spread of customer types. What they have in common is that they are

This case was prepared by Dr Cliff Bowman, Cranfield School of Management, as a basis for class discussion rather than to illustrate effective or ineffective handling of an administrative situation.

Year End December 1996	Actual	
	(£)	**(£)**
Product sales		819,327.01
Purchases		573,789.86
		245,537.15
Warehouse and distribution:		
Payroll – Warehouse	17,834.72	
Rent	15,000.00	
Rates, repairs, insurance	11,001.98	
Depreciation	5,114.15	
Payroll – Delivery	11,638.55	
Van running costs	6,116.93	
Carriage	14,786.74	
Van hire	4,968.36	
Total		86,461.43
Gross profit		159,075.72
Administration:		
Payroll – Sales	31,277.57	
Car running costs	1,822.80	
Car depreciation	2,312.52	
Loss on sale of motor vehicle	778.65	
Marketing	8,743.09	
Telephone	4,388.09	
Miscellaneous	775.08	
Payroll – Administration	36,977.34	
Light and heat	1,462.93	
Car running costs	3,366.47	
Car depreciation	750.00	
Bank charges	2,893.88	
Legal and professional	515.00	
Audit and accounting	3,900.00	
Post and stationery	4,714.03	
Training/consultancy	1,295.21	
Miscellaneous	4,029.36	
Bad debts	3,772.49	
Holding company charges	2,650.00	
Interest	3,478.87	
Total		119,903.38
Net profit		39,172.34

Figure C1.1 *Profit and loss account for SJM*

local to SJM's warehouse, they are visited by an SJM sales
representative, and deliveries are made by SJM's own van.

C   *Out-of-area customers* These are customers that have been
acquired through telesales effort. Delivery is by national carrier,
and there is no sales rep visiting them.

D   *Small national groups* These are large buyers that have a chain of
hotels, or restaurants. SJM sell direct to the central buyer
located at the firm's HQ. Delivery is by national carrier or by
SJM's van. The largest customer has a chain of eight hotels
situated mainly in the south of England.

E   *Large national groups* For example, any major hotel, pub or
restaurant chain (e.g. Trust House Forte). Steve believes that
SJM do not have the capability to serve this size of client.

SJM focus their effort on groups B, C and D. Steve explains that within
these groupings customers fall into one of three categories:

1.   Hotel and restaurant (accounting for 50 per cent of current
sales).

2.   Quick service caterers like cafés, takeaways, industrial
caterers, schools, hospitals (35 per cent of current sales).

3.   Non-caterers: industry/commerce, food manufacturers,
wholesale companies (15 per cent of sales).

Competitors

The main national suppliers are Whitacker/ACS owned by Bunzl Plc,
Autobar, Key Catering, Provend (recently floated), and Swan Mill (a
manufacturer selling direct). Within the region served by SJM there are
an additional twenty suppliers, but the competitor Steve fears most is
Whittle and Heap. Set up by two thirty-year-old salesmen from Autobar, this partnership has grown to £2.5m. sales since 1984. By remain-
ing loyal to their suppliers (Kimberly Clark, Huntsman and Duni), Steve
believes that they have been able to be very aggressive on price. Whittle
and Heap currently employ four sales reps covering London and the
south of England. They also use telesales effectively, and all deliveries
are made in their own vehicles. Their product range includes beverages

and cleaning products, but they are presently relatively inactive in the Bedford area.

Steve attributes Whittle and Heap's growth to a combination of factors. Part of their success is due to sticking to a restricted set of suppliers; they have been able to benefit from larger bulk-ordering discounts. Also, they have been prepared to accept lower margins than SJM, particularly on high-use products. Dave Whittle will develop an area himself before recruiting a sales person to look after it. If there are problems, Dave moves in to sort it out. They tend to recruit sales people aged 25–30; they drive them hard and are quite ruthless in getting rid of people who can't stand the pace. They have recently been successful in securing low-margin volume contracts with hospitals and universities.

Product range

SJM offer the standard range of disposables: napkins, table covers and skirts, coasters and laceware, candles, bar accessories, party products (balloons, crackers, hats), plates, cutlery, cups, straws, paper towels, toilet rolls, refuse sacks. Partly due to demands from customers and partly as a response to Whittle and Heap, SJM have extended their product range to include cleaning materials (detergents, bleach, disinfectants, polish) and beverages (coffee, tea, whiteners, sugar sachets, etc.). On average, they keep about 1,000 lines in stock. They will also supply customized prints on napkins, cups, sachets, etc. They use a freelance graphic designer for the artwork.

Suppliers

SJM endeavour to supply all their customers' needs from stock held at their site in Bedford. This two-storey building houses all the stock, and the offices. Routine stock-ordering is done by the warehouse manager Shane Cooper. The warehouse receives handwritten orders from the sales office, and makes up the orders for delivery.

Kimberly Clark are a major supplier to the trade. They are very professional in their dealings with customers like SJM, and have recently introduced a discount structure that classifies customers into one of three bands. SJM are in the low-discount band; each higher band means that the buyer gets about 6 per cent lower prices.

SJM have tended to shop around to get the lowest prices from suppliers. Steve does not believe that the customer can distinguish any quality differences between Kimberly Clark's premium-priced products (e.g. hand towels) and lower-priced, unbranded "economy" products. For example, a barrel roll of paper for use in washrooms would cost £22 from Kimberly Clark, whereas an unbranded roll might cost as little as £12 from another supplier. Manufacturers like Kimberly Clark and Jamont promote their products with the end customer (e.g. the hotel chain) and they offer free dispensers so long as their products are used to refill them. Other suppliers include Deeko (now part of Jamont, a US-based corporation), Duni (napkins etc.), Huntsman and Linpac (who supply polystyrene boxes), Imalpak and Polarap (disposable cups etc.). SJM also buy napkins from a small local manufacturer. SJM's relationships with suppliers may have suffered a little, first, because of their tendency to shop around for the best prices, and secondly, because SJM had some problems paying bills in the depths of the recent recession. Most suppliers are prepared to offer special price support to favoured clients to enable them to secure or retain important accounts.

Items that are more peripheral to SJM's range (e.g. dishwashing powder) they buy locally from a wholesaler.

Staff and organization

The current organization structure is set out in the Figure C1.2. There are only nine employees, four of those being part-time. The field salesman, Barry Kirk, has only just joined the business to replace the previous salesman, Bill French. Bill was involved in a car crash in the summer of 1996, which has unfortunately left him unable to drive a car. This has been a blow for the business, as well as being a personal tragedy for Bill. Bill was largely responsible for building up the group business (category D above), and Steve was grooming him to take over the business when he retired in six years' time. Barry Kirk, aged 52, was made redundant from an animal feed company, and although he has over thirty years' sales experience, Steve considers his lack of product knowledge to be a disadvantage. Also, Steve is concerned that Barry

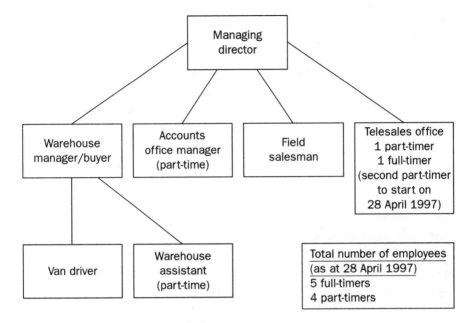

Figure C1.2 *Management structure for SJM*

lacks drive and energy. As Steve puts it: "I see too much of him; he should be on the road, but he's too fond of chatting in the office."

The warehouse manager Shane Cooper is an ex-army sergeant who joined the firm in 1990. He has a good understanding of stock and stock control, and is able to deal directly with suppliers for routine ordering of stock. Steve and Shane jointly negotiate prices with suppliers. Steve has some concerns about Shane's attitude to customers. Shane has a part-time assistant, and the van driver also reports to him.

The sales office is staffed by Vicky Hailey and Kay McCarthy. Vicky was recruited initially following an advertisement for telesales staff. Steve was impressed by her style over the phone, but was rather taken aback when she appeared at interview. Steve describes her as an ex-hippy, and he admits that he employed her despite some misgivings. However, Vicky has proved to be an outstanding salesperson. She is responsible for building up the telesales business from nothing four years ago to £250,000 today (category C above), as well as maintaining relationships with existing local and national chain clients. Kay, who works full-time, describes herself as "a bit of a plodder", but customers like her for her honesty and efficiency. Kay believes the customers expect items to be in stock, but if you have run out, that it is important to tell the customer, and not send the order out with an item missing. The current wage for a telesales person is about £5 an hour; bonuses can boost monthly income by up to £50 per week.

One of the problems facing the telesales operation is that Vicky spends a lot of her time now dealing with the customer base she has built up, leaving limited time for cold-calling prospective customers. A third telesales person (PT) has recently been recruited.

The order-taking process is straightforward. Customers either phone in for a repeat order, or they are contacted on a routine basis. Vicky or Kay call up the client's details on the computer, and check their preferred items. If they have time they might also check whether the customer requires other supplies. The scribbled notes from the phone call are then transcribed in longhand on to an order form. These are collected regularly by Shane, or his assistant, for dispatch. If the customer is local, the sales office can indicate the day the van will call (usually within three days); for out-of-area customers, once the urgency of the order is established, an appropriate national carrier is contacted.

SJM produce a brochure containing a list of products (in two colours, with some line drawings), and they produce full-colour promotional leaflets for particular campaigns (e.g. ordering for Christmas stock).

The future

Steve would like to build sales to about £2m. turnover in the next three or four years. He believes this will give him a better chance of getting a good price for the business should he decide to retire. He thinks the future of the business lies with group sales (category D). Although they only have four of these customers, each customer has between five and ten outlets. Negotiation is done centrally on prices, and then each unit places its orders separately with SJM. The business is attractive because, although it requires a good deal of sales effort to get it in the first place, thereafter it is just a question of maintaining the relationship. And, so far, all four group customers have themselves expanded, which leads to increased sales for SJM without any sales costs. Steve also believes the out-of-area customers (category C) have considerable potential provided suitable telesales personnel can be recruited.

Gross margins are lower on group sales (about 24 per cent), local area (category B) earning 30 per cent, and telesales 32 per cent. Steve has always tried to maintain margins, even in the depths of the recession. He used to believe that the ideal business has high margins and low turnover, advice he picked up years ago from a successful Scottish businessman of his acquaintance. However, the recession changed his mind about this because SJM was very exposed to aggressive competition. The field sales force had to be cut from four to one during the recession as sales volumes plummeted (Steve had to trade in his Jaguar for a modest Cavalier!). Steve feels that a good salesman can get the business, but that it is too easy to lose it on price. All it takes is for, say, a sales visit from Whitfield and Heap, who are prepared to supply some items at cost, and all the efforts of the salesman are undermined. Steve thinks that Whitfield and Heap must be working on much lower prices, but they could be compensating for these with lower supply costs.

Steve feels the business is vulnerable to a concerted attack by Whitfield and Heap. In fact, he cannot understand why they have not moved in to his "patch" already. He misses his management meetings with Bill French, and feels there is no one he can discuss the future of the business with. He knows he should be "out there" helping to drum up business, but he is not a natural salesman, preferring to limit his visits to customers to when they are really needed (usually to resolve a problem). His strategy of focusing on the group accounts has stalled with Bill leaving the firm, so where is the extra £1m. business going to come from?

Further reading

There are a large number of strategy textbooks on the market. For further development of the ideas in this book, particularly for those interested in corporate strategy, I suggest that you should read C. Bowman and D. Faulkner, *Competitive and Corporate Strategy* (Irwin, 1997). For a more mainstream treatment of strategy, see G. Johnson and K. Scholes, *Exploring Corporate Strategy*, 4th edn (Prentice Hall, 1997).

For a fuller discussion of the resource-based perspective, Rob Grant's book *Contemporary Strategy Analysis* (Blackwells, 1995) is excellent.

For those interested in exploring issues in organization structure, Henry Mintzberg's *Structure in Fives* (Prentice Hall, 1983) elaborates the approach I summarized in Chapter 6.

The role of the corporate centre is addressed in M. Goold, A. Campbell and M. Alexander, *Corporate Level Strategy* (Wiley, 1994).

Alliances are explored in some depth in D. Faulkner, *Strategic Alliances: Cooperating to Compete* (McGraw-Hill, 1995).

Index

acquisition, 175, 180–3
alliances, 175–7, 178–9
appropriability, 43–4

belief in strategy, 165–8
beliefs, 125–6, 135–8
blinkered strategy, 9–11, 126
brand loyalty, 78
brands, 46–7
budgets, 2
business level strategy, 5
buyers
  bargaining power of, 79

CEO, 149, 169
change, 145–171
  barriers to, 159–61, 169
  and culture, 145–7
  and mission statement, 154–5
  and project management, 157–8
cognitive processes, 125, 135–8
commitment to strategy, 6, 161–4,
    168–9, 170
  belief and confidence, 165–8
competences, 42, 48–51, 64–6
  champions, 156–7
  core and key, 64
  and corporate strategy, 172–3
  imitability, 71
competitive environment, 70–97
competitive imitation, 30, 43, 45, 67
  role of know–how, 51
competitor reactions, 66–7
  analysis of, 92–5
confidence in setting strategy, 12–16
configurations, 115
consultant's strategy, 8–9, 147
controls, 129–130
coordination, 100–3

corporate strategy, 3, 4, 172–89
  corporate centre, 172
  corporate logic, 4, 187
cost strategies, 56–63
  crude cost–cutting, 61, 117, 164
  lowest cost producer, 24
  risks of, 27
crisis, 13, 148, 165–6
cross-functional teams, 158
culture, 122–44
  and change, 145–6
  and strategy, 124–6
customer matrix, 20–41
  constructing the matrix, 36–40
  movements in, 21–36, 42–3
customer needs, 71–2
customer stereotypes, 40

demand, 71
  drivers of, 71–2
  effects of declining, 76
direct supervision, 100
diversification, 174–5
diversity, 111–13, 118
durability of resources, 44

economies of scale, 35, 56, 59, 77–8,
  179
economies of scope, 57, 59, 180
empowerment, 16, 129, 155
entrepreneurial organization, 113–14
entry barriers, 24, 77–9
environment
  analysis of, 70–97
  dynamism and organizational
    structure, 107–111
experience
  barrier to entry, 78
  cost advantages of, 35, 59

experience (*continued*)
  and market share, 57
  personal, 166–8

factor costs, 58, 59
first-mover advantage, 66–7
five forces framework, *see* structural
     analysis of industries
fixed costs, 76
force-field analysis, 159–61
functional structure, 99, 104–6
  and change, 156
  cross–functional teams, 158

generic strategies, 20, 34
grouping staff, 127–8

holding company, 4
horizontal integration, 177, 180

know-how, 48–9, 50, 53–4

imitability, *see also* competitive
     imitation drivers of, 72–3
impoverished strategy, 6–8, 126
indoctrination, 136
informal networks, 128
innovative organization, 113, 115
intuition, 17
intuitive core, 11

life cycle of industry, 85–8

machine bureaucracy, 102, 113, 114
make/buy/ally matrix, 176–7
management styles, 130–2
managerial efficiencies, 57–8
matrix structure, 112–13, 120, 185–6
means-end analysis, 52–3, 54–6
middle line, 103
mission statements, 7, 149–56
  and action, 152–5
  guidelines, 150–1
mutual adjustment, 100

not-for-profit organizations, 185–7

operating core, 103
operational level strategy, 5
organizational processes, 103–4,
     126–7
organization structure, 98–121
  and change, 156, 158–9

paradigm, 136–8
parenting role, 173
perceived price, 21
perceived use value, 20, 28–30
  dimensions of, 28–9, 37
  PUV profile, 29
PEST analysis, 89–92
planning
  problems with, 2, 7, 122
  as ritual, 7–8
power, 128–9
  and dependence, 129
price
  as a measure of perceived value,
     23
  wars, 24–5
price cutting strategy, 23–7, 35
  risks of, 27
prioritizing, 161–3
product surround, 62
professional organization, 113,
     114–15
project management, 157–8

realized strategy, 126, 139–40
recipe, 13, 136–8
replicability of resources, 47
required strategy, 11–12
resource-based theory, 20, 43–8
resources, 48–9
rewards, 129–30, 163
risk, 174, 177
rituals, 133–5
rivalry, 74–7
routines, 132–3, 138–9
rules of the game, 88

segments of demand, 22, 60, 70, 71
  competing across several, 64–6
self-confidence, 165–8, 188–9
specialization, 99–100, 105
  functional, 99, 104–6
  grouping, 127–8
standardization, 101–2, 105
stories, 133
strategic apex, 103
strategic business units, 3, 172
strategic detail, 68, 133, 166–8
strategic drift, 13
strategy
  business level, 5
  corporate, 3, 4
  and culture, 122

strategy (*continued*)
  debates, 2
  definition of, 168
  key questions in, 5
  levels of, 3
  operational level, 5–6
  overload, 8
strategy processes, 6–12, 147
  process prescriptions, 11–12
strategy and structure, 98–121
  contingency approach, 106–118
structural analysis of industries,
    73–85
  advantages of, 84–5
substitutes, 80–4
suppliers
  bargaining power of, 79–80, 81–2

support staff, 103
switching costs, 76–7, 78, 80
symbols, 133
synergy, 4, 118, 120, 183–8
systems, 48–9

tacit knowledge, 49, 53, 68
task complexity, 107, 111–13
technostructure, 103
transferability of resources, 45

values, 125, 135–8
vertical integration, 177, 179

X-inefficiency, 57

zones of debate, 9–11